Successful Ethical Decision Making

Successful Ethical Decision Making

Get What You Want Without Getting In Trouble

Michael Tate Barkley
with John Henry Glover

2007

Published by Critical Communications, LLC
14090 Southwest Freeway, Suite 308
Sugar Land, Texas 77478

Successful Ethical Decision Making

Table of Contents

Acknowledgements

I started the process of writing this book as a solitary endeavor. Like most of my solitary endeavors, I quickly became distracted and unproductive. With me, in almost all things, it does take a village. This book is no exception.

I want to offer thanks to those of my village. I want to thank Patti McKenna who patiently transcribed numerous audio meanderings of mine so as to provide an initial workable manuscript. Jim Jacobus for persuading me that now is the time to write a book. To my law partner and dear friend, Steve Bain, who persuaded me that now is the time to finish the book. Further, Steve exemplifies the idea of Integrity that I discuss in the book.

I thank Jenni Fann, Cindy Wooten, and probably others for typing, formatting and numbering all the scribbles and scratches I called edits.

To Lisa Russek, who has advised, counseled, edited, organized and orchestrated the entire process of getting this book completed and finalized.

To my dear, dear friend, Fairan Jones, who contributed with edits, research and most of all an unyielding friendship which keeps me together in all of my pursuits.

I thank my students at the University of Houston who continue to inspire, annoy, and entertain me to this day. Each class with all of you gives me purpose and joy.

Finally, to my friend John Glover, for organizing, modifying and finessing my text. Your gift of making the book more dynamic and readable was indispensable. Thank you.

INTRODUCTION

We are all creatures of habit; I am no exception. Everyday, I wake up and follow my morning ritual. First, I start the coffee, and then I retrace yesterday's steps to the front door where I pick up the <u>Houston Chronicle</u>. Before I get ready for work, I take time to sit down and enjoy my coffee and catch up on the news. This has been my routine for years. The newspaper has always been my preferred connection to the world. For me, the printed word is more credible, more manageable and less intense. There is an ease and predictability to learning by reading. Reading the newspaper and news magazines is how I have learned since I was a boy. It seems the older I become, the less time I have available. My cherished time with the morning paper seems to become less and less at a time the news seems to become more and more.

I don't think I need to tell you how much news there is; the media has found a way to bring breaking news and events into our lives as quickly as they happen. Through radio, television, e-mail, Internet, text messages, and the printed word, we are bombarded daily with more information than our minds (at least my mind) can process. Interestingly, the more we are exposed to it, the less we seem to be affected by it.

As I sit here this morning with coffee in hand, I find myself wondering how and why it is that I am sometimes numb to the news reports which would have angered, motivated, or thrilled me some years ago. What I realize during this searching saddens me. Times have changed. It is common to hear tales of tragedy, violence, and deceit. Unfortunately, it is indeed a rarity to pick up a newspaper without being inundated with articles depicting crime, conflict, or malfeasance of some sort. As such events become commonplace, they become familiar and less shocking. I begin to accept them as a part of my daily life, as much a part as my morning coffee or daily newspaper. I see this change in others as well.

These subtle shifts in attitude have a profound and significant impact on our perceptions and behavior. After a period of time, we become a product of the information we receive. I see this not only in my law practice, but also in the class room. I have been a practicing attorney for nearly two decades and I have learned as much about people in the practice of law as I have following the news. In addition to my law practice, I teach at the University of Houston. Among my classes are Communications Law and Ethics, and Business and Professional Communications. It is not a job undertaken for the money. I teach quite simply because I derive a great deal of pleasure from working with my students. I probably get more out of it than they do.

My students frequently impress and amaze me; yet, there are times when they cause me a great deal of concern. They, too, are a product of the information they receive and the ever-changing world around them. They have grown up amidst corporate and political scandals, where high profile leaders are no longer role models. Unethical and unlawful behavior dominates their world. It often worries me that my students receive so much exposure to unethical behavior and wrong doing.

Is there a culprit? Is there a reason why our personal and professional lives are becoming inundated with reports of unethical behavior? I believe many factors have impacted how businesses and people in general make decisions today. Twenty first century economics and culture presents a myriad of challenges for all decision makers. The seemingly constant flow of negative news is but one factor. There is also a demand for ever more information and access to information. Correspondingly, we feel obligated to know more and be constantly in contact. Technology has made us accessible 24 hours a day, seven days a week, anywhere in the world, at all times. The expectation is humans should function as technology functions. Today, communications are instantaneous and immediate, creating the expectation that responses and decisions should be simultaneous. As a consequence, our time for thoughtful deliberation in decision making has suffered.

This sense of access and overload with information and the technology which delivers it is a natural function of our time. Our information age has also substantially changed the economic condition in which we live. Economic flexibility has essentially created financial insecurity. This feeling of financial insecurity has made daily living more difficult, further exacerbating our ability to make thoughtful ethical decisions. People deal with those challenges everyday. We are continually informed of issues relating to globalization and outsourcing. There is a constant demand for greater productivity in every economic sector.

From the early 1970's until 1995, non-farm business productivity growth averaged a meager 1.5% per year. But between 1995 and 2001, even as the 1990's era expansion ripened, productivity grew at a remarkable rate: about 2.5% per year
-<u>Fortune Magazine</u>, September 04, 2006, "The Productivity Watch" Vol. 154 No. 5

The consequences of our present reality are apparent. Job insecurity may cause one person to falsify an employment application or usurp a colleague's idea. For example, an applicant may embellish his education a bit to look more desirable to an employer.

A study by <u>resumedoctor.com</u>, a resume advisory service, found that nearly 43% of more than 1,100 resumes it checked for dates of employment, job titles and education contained at least one significant inaccuracy. Nearly 13% contained two or more inaccuracies. — <u>Miami Herald</u>, June 26, 2006

They are nervous the first time; but if they don't get caught, they do it again. The more they do it, the easier it becomes. Eventually, it becomes routine. Applicants no longer think about it; their little white lie has become accepted. The "little" misrepresentation has become an accepted, yet false, part of their thought processes, affecting their thinking and the truth they have come to know. Their fundamental sense of ethics has been altered, though only slightly. However, this slight alteration grows even larger as the demands of daily living become even larger. This affects people from all walks of life.

Marilee Jones, MIT's dean of admissions who has spoken out nationally against the craze over beefing up teens' resumes, has resigned after 28 years at the school for misrepresenting her academic degrees, university officials said today.

Jones listed on her resume that she had degrees from Albany Medical College, Union College, and Rensselaer Polytechnic Institute, but she had no degrees from any of those schools, said MIT chancellor Phillip Clay.

In a statement posted on the Massachusetts Institute of Technology's website, Jones said she did not "have the courage to correct my resume" when she applied in 1997 for her current job, where she has become perhaps the most prominent admissions director in the country. Jones has kept a popular blog and spoken widely about restoring the joys of youth to young people obsessed with their resumes.
—<u>The Boston Globe</u>, April 26, 2007.

The last two generations have witnessed a changing landscape of priorities. There is most significantly a constant pursuit of money. In my law practice, almost all of our cases are about money. With my students, they overwhelmingly mention money as their top priority upon graduation. Affluence is emphasized in every area of life from television programs to self-help seminars and is highlighted in many social circles.

Now, please allow me to correct any early misconceptions. I do believe that affluence is good. Life is much easier with money than without money, and people have long since understood this. However, it is my observation that what was once a commonly appreciated priority has become a warped obsession for many.

As all these challenges press upon us, there is an increasing number willing to cut corners to gain money, access, acknowledgement, or a sense of security. Unfortunately, the first corners usually cut are the ethical ones.

> *White collar crime refers to illegal, non-violent activity committed in business situations by individuals, groups or corporations for financial gain. Most white collar crimes are associated with some type of fraud, often involving a lending institution, such as a bank or insurance agency. Examples of white collar crimes include: antitrust fraud, bankruptcy fraud, bribery, computer fraud, credit card fraud, counterfeiting, embezzlement, identity fraud, insider trading, insurance fraud, kickbacks and money laundering, obstruction of justice, perjury and price fixing. According to National Fraud Center statistics, the costs associated with these economic crimes has increased by twenty fold from $5 billion in 1970 to $100 billion in 1990.* "White Collar Crime Statistics" www.onlinelawyersource. com (2006).

> *According to the National White Collar Crime Center, approximately one in three households is the victim of white collar crime with only 41% of these incidents being reported.* "White Collar Crime Statistics" www. onlinelawyersource.com (2006).

I sincerely believe that inside most people there is a moral compass which guides them. They know right versus wrong and try to do the right thing at work and in their daily lives. When people stray from their integrity and sense of ethics, it is likely due to the fear of failure and economic insecurity. This fear is exacerbated by ever-changing and demanding technology which has created not just an economic condition, but a social condition of rapid decision making.

Yes, times have indeed changed, and along with it, so has our ethical landscape. After considerable thought, it is my opinion that economic anxiety, technology, and the media have significantly heightened the perceived pressure for immediate decision making.

We are a product of our changing times. Still, I don't believe that people have changed — they remain inherently the same. My observations and interactions with people, as an attorney, teacher, and a fellow human being, have given me some insight into the causes and reasons for some of the changes in attitudes and behaviors our society has undergone. Through a variety of interactions with others, whether they were positive or negative, I have learned something.

Through this book, I hope to share some of these personal lessons with you. Simply put, it is my view that widespread exposure to negative news, the explosive growth of communication, the pervasiveness and immediacy of technology, the perceived need for immediate answers, and economic anxieties have significantly altered our ethical culture. Throughout it all, however, I have found that people who consistently prioritize the best interests of others over their own are the happiest and quite often most successful people. These successful individuals are always acting in someone else's best interest. Stated another way, these people are ultimately getting what they want WITHOUT getting in trouble. Our western laws refer to these individuals as *fiduciaries* or that they possess a fiduciary obligation.

> **Fiduciary:** from the Latin term fiduciarius meaning holding in trust. As a noun, it refers to a person to whom property or power is entrusted for the benefit of another.
> *www.dictionary.com Unabridged, based upon the Random House Unabridged Dictionary, Random House Inc. (2006).*

I have come to believe that the three core principles of a fiduciary are the perfect guideposts for conducting one's life. These principles can be used by anyone, regardless of profession, vocation, or circumstances.

For our purposes, what is a principle? My friend, motivational speaker, Jim Jacobus,defines priniciple as "something that can be used by anybody, anywhere, anytime for anything." Frankly, the principles in this book should apply in virtually any decision making situation.

They are as valuable in one's professional career as they are in one's personal life. I hope these concepts will provide a simple guideline to follow which will be helpful in all parts of your life. I firmly believe that following these principles will help you...

Get what you want...
WITHOUT getting in trouble!

Chapter One

THE HORNS OF A DILEMMA

IMAGINE THAT YOU are a senior staff news reporter for a major urban newspaper. This morning, you received a rather enticing invitation from a Juvenile Court District Judge granting you an exclusive interview at his home. As a leading advocate of juvenile rights and juvenile justice, the judge has been a high-profile public figure in the community for over 20 years. However, this judge was recently charged on several counts of aggravated sexual assault of a minor under the age of 14, as well as possession of child pornography. Publicly, the judge has denied all charges and allegations. He has entered a plea of not guilty and has been released on bond. The judge's trial is scheduled to begin tomorrow morning. [1]

When he extended the invitation for the personal interview, the judge mentioned that he has certain restrictions which he will disclose after you arrive at his house this evening. Accordingly, prior to beginning the interview, the judge states that he will speak with you and give you permission to print his story, on one condition: You must agree that you will not publish the article until after 5:00 p.m. the following day. He further states that you are also not at liberty to discuss the interview or your meeting with anyone until after 5:00 p.m. the following day. To enforce these restrictions, the judge requires you to sign a written contract stating the terms of the agreement before starting the interview. The executed contract states that it binds you and your newspaper to its terms.

During the course of the interview, the judge surprisingly confesses to certain allegations of sexual abuse of children. He further advises that the acts were consensual. The judge expresses sincere regret for his misconduct and informs you it will never happen again. The interview concludes at 9:00 p.m. As you leave, the judge reminds you of the terms of the contract, and he provides you with a copy. Then, the judge unexpectedly informs you that he will be committing suicide at midnight!

What will you do? What are the ethical, moral, legal, and practical implications?

As a professor at the University of Houston, I teach a course entitled Communications Law and Ethics. This was a dilemma I presented to my students. Every semester, I present similar ethical dilemmas concerning various issues to my class.

In one specific instance, I began the course with this particular situation and I gave the students 15 minutes to discuss it among themselves before sharing their thoughts with me and the rest of the class. After hearing their responses, I was amazed as I became aware that my students had so many different opinions regarding their ethical duty. In addition, I found it interesting that their course of study or major heavily influenced them as they determined their ethical duty. For example, it was quite clear that many of my journalism students believed that the publication of such sensational, sensitive, and critical information was more important than any deal or agreement. It was quite clear their "first to the story" competitive juices were flowing. On the other hand, some students were more concerned with the contract with regards only to its financial ramifications for breaching its terms, not only for themselves but also for the shareholders of the newspaper. Another handful, a very distinct minority was vehement that the Judge's intent to commit suicide was the most defining variable. In their mind, preventing him from performing this act was paramount.

A flood of different responses poured in from my students. During their discussion, I sat back and quietly listened to my students go back and forth as they expressed their opinions. Each group would push and pull at the others as they argued their ethical sensibility. I have to tell you that their opinions were varied and quite intense.

While listening, I noticed how quickly many of these students overlooked their personal commitment altogether, focusing most of their attention on how they could best control the situation. As for others, it was as if, upon his confession, the judge had lost all entitlement to consideration and his pending suicide had little bearing on the issue. A select few, however, continued to argue for suicide prevention. I listened to the thoughts and opinions of the class and waited, but there was not one single student who said, "But I gave this man *my word*"!

What would a fiduciary have to do?

Chapter Two

CONSIDERING THE CONTEXT

I am privileged to teach talented and impressive students. However, their responses took me aback, and I pondered where we were as individuals, as humans, in terms of our sense of ethics as we live and work on a daily basis.

In this instance, I purposely gave my students an admitted child molester—a bad person by mainstream U.S. standards, who by his own admission, was a potential danger to the most vulnerable members of our society. Even worse, the judge had been a proponent and advocate for the very persons he abused. But, there were other considerations. If the judge did commit suicide, what would be the impact? Would his suicide bring him justice? Would it satisfy and bring closure to his victims?

If the judge decided not to follow through on the suicide, how would this impact the trial? Would it affect his victims or the potential legal exposure to the reporter, the paper, and others?

In this instance, the dilemma that was confronted by my students, as well as the reporter in our scenario, is one of innumerable ethical situations that could arise. Although at times likely less intense, similar ethical dilemmas are confronted everyday by persons in varying social, economic, political, and personal situations. Yet, more often than we expect, we see unethical and uncivil behavior take place in every venue of our lives. We see it on television, we see it in our workplace, we see it in our schools, and there are times we even see it in our families. Unfortunately, all too often it seems to surround us.

The reactions and discussions that played out in my ethics class in many ways reflected our times. My students' views were reflective of the specific situation which they confronted at the moment. As you recall, I gave them only 15 minutes to consider their dilemma and decide. Each had to deal with a flood of conflicting emotions and concerns. The facts of the situation and the environment were out of their control. The only facts they had to work with were those I gave them. More importantly, I did not give my students a protocol or a roadmap for making such a decision. Each student was forced to rely upon his or her own sense of self and thus consider only factors which had the greatest personal influence on each of them.

Like all people, my students are not immune to being influenced by their situation and environment. They are also products of the information that they receive. Each day they are inundated with news or information of some kind. Whether it is text messages, the Internet, newspaper articles, e-mails, 24-hour television news, radio, telephone, satellite or cable, we are constantly being inundated with information, much of which has been sensationalized. You and I have watched a society that has been influenced by Watergate, Iran Contra, the Monica Lewinsky scandal, Congressman Mark Foley, and high-level government cover-ups. We have all witnessed the exposure of corporate corruption at MCI WorldCom and the infamous Enron scandal. In each of these instances people gave their word to others, but we later learned they did not keep it.

As a result, it appears that most people, including myself, become more insensitive to the issues around them. As a society, we've become numb with overexposure. This numbing or desensitization takes hold and our sense of responsibility to others begins to erode.

Enron Code of Ethics, July 2000 — www.TheSmokingGun.com

Business Ethics
Employees of Enron Corp., its subsidiaries, and its affiliated companies (collectively the "Company") are charged with conducting their business affairs in accordance with the highest ethical standards. An employee shall not conduct himself or herself in a manner which directly or indirectly would be detrimental to the best interests of the Company or in a manner which would bring to the employee financial gain separately derived as a direct consequence of his or her employment with the Company. Moral as well as legal obligations will be fulfilled openly, promptly, and in a manner which will reflect pride on the Company's name.

Products and services of the Company will be of the highest quality and as represented. Advertising and promotion will be truthful, not exaggerated or misleading.

Agreements, whether contractual or verbal, will be honored. No bribes, bonuses, kickbacks, lavish entertainment, or gifts will be given or received in exchange for special position, price, or privilege.

Employees will maintain the confidentiality of the Company's sensitive or proprietary information and will not use such information for their personal benefit.

Employees shall refrain, both during and after their employment, from publishing any oral or written statements about the Company or any of its' officers, employees, agents, or representatives that are slanderous, libelous, or defamatory; or that disclose private or confidential information about their business affairs; or that constitute an intrusion into their seclusion or private lives; or that give rise to unreasonable publicity about their private lives; or that place them in a false light before the public; or that constitute a misappropriation of their name or likeness.

Relations with the Company's many publics —customers, stockholders, governments, employees, suppliers, press, and bankers —will be conducted in honesty, candor and fairness.

Chapter Three

MEDIA: WHAT IS THE CONTEXT?

The media significantly impacts many areas of our lives. But, just what role does the media play in decision making?

Despite what many would expect or believe, media members are not there to teach us how to be honest or to provide us with ethical training; their job is simply to report items of news and interest to the public. Often, these items of news and interest involve wrongdoing and ethical dilemmas. Commonly, a well-balanced and well documented news item is prepared by an ethical and thoughtful journalist. Yet, slanted and sensationalized news items are prevalent and often more visible today.

The fact of the matter is that the media and news coverage are too often overflowing with accounts of wrongdoings in society, some of which are clearly *sensationalized*. It is difficult to find a newspaper or nightly news program which isn't monopolized by tragedy, violence, and corruption. This constant and repeated exposure to overtly negative news has made such events common in our lives. Rarely are these types of reports countered with heartwarming stories depicting honesty and goodness in our fellow man. Thus, we are left with the impression that dishonesty is a commonly accepted practice. By repeatedly spotlighting the negative, we virtually eliminated the value of the positive.

This prevalence of sensational impropriety is exacerbated by the ever increasing television viewing habit of Americans.

During the 2005-06 TV season, the average household in the U.S. tuned into television an average of 8 hours and 1 minute per day. This is 2.7% higher than the previous season, 12.5% higher than 10 years ago, and the highest levels ever reported since television viewing was first measured by Nielsen Media Research in the 1950's. Source: Neilsen Media Research (www. neilsenmedia.com)

As a whole, we watch more TV than ever. The television programs being watched all too often depict the less than exemplary conduct of people from all walks of life.

Big businesses and corporations are not immune to negative media attention. The recent slew of corporate corruption scandals received their fair share of attention. There was intense coverage of Martha Stewart's insider trading and her subsequent imprisonment. This was augmented by the extensive coverage of the fall of Enron and the almost overt fraud committed at MCI WorldCom. Conversely, the profiles of socially responsible corporations, such as Vermont's Green Mountain Roasters Coffee Company, Malden Mills, and numerous others, receive slight coverage.

Even someone as famous and as admired as Oprah Winfrey is not immune from the effects of dishonesty. She was forced to publicly withdraw her support and recommendation for a book written by James Frey called A Million Little Pieces. It appears that the author had embellished certain aspects of his "true story," and his credibility was questioned and investigated. Oprah experienced significant personal and professional embarrassment as a result. Events like this affect all of us.

High profile events such as these become a daily occurrence in our lives, just like the dilemma involving the Juvenile Judge which I posed in Chapter One. My young class members have grown up in a culture swarming with such news and similar events. It is a part of their daily lives, as well as ours. As my students are also a part of my daily life, I've observed firsthand their stresses as they are pulled in many directions. Like most of us, they have obligations to their employers, their families, the law, their faith or religion, and to themselves and their sense of who they really are. I continually recommend to my students to take a step back from the media inundating their lives, to take a deep breath, and to consider what kind of people they really want to be.

Chapter Four

TECHNOLOGY: REACH OUT AND TOUCH SOMEONE...24/7

Most of us experience life and conduct ourselves through some manner of communication and interaction. There are multiple forms of communication, and still even more ways in which people interact. We speak, write, signal, gesture, and even smile as a means of communication. Technology has further expanded our methods of communication to realms which were unimaginable just 20 years ago. As technology grows, we are constantly required to learn how to use some new device. Frequently, these devices are a means of communication. Like many of you, on a typical day I am contacted through my home, office, cell phone, email, text message, facsimile, snail mail, certified mail, knocks on the door, and word of mouth. The use of all these forms in one single day is not uncommon. On most days, I take little notice.

Internet access in the United States

As of 2004, three out of four *Americans* have **Internet access in the United States**, with more than 50% of these being <u>broadband</u> connections. 74.9% of Americans living in households with a <u>fixed line phone</u> have home access to the <u>Internet</u>. This amounts to 204,307 million Americans. This is up from 66% a year earlier.

From Wikipedia, the free encyclopedia based on a <u>March 18, 2004</u> press release from <u>Nielsen//NetRatings</u>.

The number of cell phone subscribers in the United States reached approximately 159 million in 2003, up from 34 million in 1995, an increase of 468% according to the <u>U.S. Census Bureau</u>, dated December 9, 2004.

As technology evolves, it appears that our behavior toward each other changes. I have discussed this topic frequently with my colleagues and many of them have noticed this as well. Technology in many respects was intended to make us more accessible, but does it really? It is my view that all too often we hide behind technology. It is easier to send an e-mail or leave a scalding or belligerent voice mail than it is to deliver that same message face to face. This technological wall creates a false sense of separation which lends itself to rapid emotional response sent without thoughtful consideration.

Another underlying problem is miscommunication. Perhaps I am a bit conventional in my thinking, but I rarely get a text message that I can actually understand. The majority of them need to be translated or decoded. Often e-mail is done so hastily that its tone is abrupt leading to unintended interpretations.

I have also observed that technology is a distraction, a means to divert our attention away from what is actually happening around us. It is difficult to be mindful and present in our own life while we are punching out a text message or scrolling through a Blackberry. This is especially evident while traveling. I make an effort to observe people whenever I am at an airport. It seems that people are afraid to be alone with their own thoughts and feelings. Almost every person I see is talking on a cell phone, checking e-mails on a Blackberry, or manipulating a laptop in some way. It also seems as if we feel it is wrong if we are not engaged in some activity.

Possibly complicating matters, the choices of those activities continue to grow. With today's technology, the methods of communication are almost unlimited.

I know some of you may be asking at this point, what does this have to do with my view of unethical behavior? For me, the answer is really quite simple. When we are willing to be distracted in our conversations and communications, we lose personal connectedness. Think about what happens when we talk on a cell phone in an elevator so that others can hear, allow our phone to ring in class, or choose to scroll through a Blackberry in an airport instead of engaging in a conversation with someone we don't yet know. All of these things make us more separate, and definitely less connected. I would strongly argue that the more separate we become from others and our community, the more willing we are to put our own interests above others.

My observations have shown me that technology can shield us from our community and from the people around us, instead of bringing us closer together and making us more accessible. As an unintended consequence, technological advances can make it easier for us to be less involved and less accountable to those around us.

Results from a recent study appear to demonstrate a declining sense of connection to others within our society. As reported in USA Today on June 22, 2006, the <u>American Sociological Review</u> published an extensive survey of Americans. The findings were somewhat disturbing. According to the study, Americans have a third fewer close friends and confidants that just two decades ago. This can be considered a sign that people may be living lonelier and more isolated lives than in the past. The average American had three people in whom to confide in matters that were important to them in 1985. In 2004, that number had dropped to two people; and more disturbing, one in four had no close confidants at all.

"You usually don't see that kind of big social change in a couple of decades" states study co-author Lyn Smith Loving, a professor of Sociology at Duke University in Durham, North Carolina,

Another factor contributing to our individual separateness and isolation was identified by Harvard Public Policy Professor, Robert D. Putnam, who wrote <u>Bowling Alone: The Collapse and Revival of American Community</u>. Stating it rather bluntly, he said that "People have more entertainment tools such as T.V., iPods, and computers so they stay at home and tune out." This is a candid observation which makes a great deal of sense to me. The more we tune out, the more isolated we become. Contributing to the problem is that the more isolated and lonelier people are, the more prone they are to act in an inconsiderate and potentially unethical manner.

Technology has obvious utility which cannot be denied. Beyond simply transmitting information, the invention, manufacture, marketing, and sales of computers, iPods, Blackberries, cell phones, and the like are vital to our nation's economy. Technology produces jobs, income, growth, and wealth. But we must be mindful this same technology can foster loneliness and isolation which can impact our ability for ethical decision making.

Chapter Five

HIGH "ECONOMIC" ANXIETY

Let us now consider "the bottom line," how this "hits us in the pocket book," or one of the other all too common clichés. We are all aware of the need and desire for money, but I believe our growing economic anxiety is one of the most powerful causes of ethical decline.

I read an interesting article in the May 2006 issue of Forbes magazine, which shared a news brief, entitled "Economic Anxiety." This commentary takes an interesting stance on the relationship and differences between our view of the economy and how it relates to recent economic data. The article asserts that there is a fundamental disconnect between one and the other. To support the claim, the following facts and figures are discussed:

> In 2005, gross domestic product was 3.5 percent which is above average, and the annual rate for the first quarter of 2006 was a robust and impressive 4.8 percent. This solid growth was further supported by the fact that job creation was also growing at approximately 2,000,000 jobs per year. However, these economic statistics were contradicted by people's perceptions of the economy. During this same time, a CBS poll indicated only a 28% approval rating of the President's handling of the economy, despite the healthy economic news.

This disconnect was further reinforced in a Parade magazine article concerning economic anxiety, dated March 12, 2006. This article agrees that the United States has enjoyed economic growth for four straight years as supported by data from the Department of Labor, Bureau of Statistics. The authors do not neglect to point out, however, that the average American family, 80 percent of them in fact, is losing ground and is actually making less money than it did four years ago because of inflation.

The same article refers to studies that indicated that the wages of the top ten percent of earners (those who make over $90,000 yearly) have increased more quickly than in any other group. The top 10% have enjoyed significant increases in financial growth, while average workers have maintained flat earnings of $27,000 per year from 1990 to 2004. Regardless of one's political views, the fact is that the majority of citizens in our country are feeling anxious about their financial future.

American families have been exposed to a barrage of media reports depicting executives of large corporations receiving huge compensations amidst countless reports of corporate scandals. Exxon has rewarded its Chief Executive Officer, Raymond Berry, with a huge compensation package, while the company itself has benefited from record profits. This occurred at the same time that gasoline prices were at an all time high putting financial pressure on most Americans. Add in scandals, such as Enron, Tyco, Adelphia, and MCI WorldCom, just to name a few, and one can almost understand why the average U.S. citizen feels he or she is fighting a losing battle. Eventually, some succumb to the notion that our society breaks into the "haves" and the "have nots." It is undoubtedly more enviable to be one of the "haves" than "have nots." Unique pressures are placed on people everyday as they realize, or at least think, that they need more money to keep their head above water or more money to meet ever greater expectations of affluence. The result is that we begin to rationalize or justify ethical oversights that help us to achieve that end. The cycle worsens as more and more people face this very real anxiety in regard to their economic position.

The Reporter in our Juvenile Judge dilemma has similar concerns. The Reporter's job could very well be in jeopardy if this dilemma is mishandled.

Chapter Six

OUR DILEMMA, OUR REALITY, AND OUR RESPONSE

The deterioration of ethical decision making is fed by incessant negative news delivered by an ever evolving technology at a time of very real economic insecurity for most people. I tried to take all of this into account while I listened to my students as they debated the right thing to do in the juvenile judge scenario.

As I sat and reflected on the wide variety of views and considerations of my students, it became apparent that they were paralyzed by indecision or were willing to accept a decisive simple conclusion without constructively struggling through a process of careful deliberation. At first, I was troubled that not one student had said, "I gave this guy my word." Later, I was more concerned by the fact that not one of my students said, "Let's take a moment to break this dilemma down and think it all the way through." What my students saw was an admitted child molester who was in a position of power and authority, a dilemma intended to elicit a strong emotional response. After taking this into account, I could not be disappointed with them nor was I surprised. Up until this point, my students had been exposed to a great deal of unethical behavior but had not likely been exposed to ethics in school. I believe that all too often, ethics or moral propriety is not taught out of fear of offending somebody. Moreover, the law is so vast and voluminous that it is impossible for anyone to take any one course and know what is appropriate or inappropriate, and I say that as an attorney. Instinct prevails with many people as to the next right thing or ethical course of action in almost any given situation. However, when you are in uncharted waters or unfamiliar professional settings, even instinct can fail sometimes.

This class, Communications Law and Ethics, was for many of my students their first experience with any kind of formal ethical training. Up until this particular day, we had focused primarily on the law, Supreme Court rulings and relevant statutes, the common law, and, of course, all the exceptions, but I had not yet focused on ethics. The students had listened to me as I used vague wording and recited broad judicial precedent to relate instances where there was deniability and avoidance of accountability. It appeared as if I had taught them relatively well. But what had I actually taught them? I had taught them theories and litigation strategies, but apparently I had not taught them a basic guideline of how to analyze an ethical duty in a challenging situation.

As a lawyer, I am aware of countless legal duties and obligations, so it came naturally to me to rely upon judicial precedent, statute, and regulation when teaching my students. But, teaching ethics in a very legalistic world is easier said than done. It seemed impossible to distill all this law into a basic guide for ethical analysis. As I attempted to figure out the proper tactic, it occurred to me that the one legal notion that seemed to fit all of these potential situations was that of a "fiduciary." This notion of a fiduciary has multiple applications, but a very straightforward approach. Simply put, the duty of a fiduciary is to place the interest of others first. It was with the fiduciary in mind that I began to teach my class ethics. It is also through the role of the fiduciary that I will explain how you can get what you want...without getting in trouble.

Chapter Seven

THE FIDUCIARY

What is a fiduciary, and what does it have to do with ethical behavior? A fiduciary is a legal term which is given to someone who is entrusted to act on behalf of another person or organization. The key principle of fiduciaries is that they must base their actions on the best interests of another, not themselves.

A fiduciary follows a higher ethical standard. An obvious example of a fiduciary is an attorney. Lawyers take an oath that they will act in the best interests of their clients. Although the legal profession from time to time has received a great deal of negative publicity, I believe most lawyers honor their obligations. And, it is safe to say that few if any professions are more highly regulated in terms of ethical conduct.

Like many of my colleagues, I frequently make recommendations to my clients which are not always in my best interest. For example, the cost of litigation is quite expensive. An attorney's fees are a prominent variable in this equation. However, it is not uncommon for me to advise my clients to make a reasonable settlement of a dispute to prevent the drain of my client's resources. If continued litigation is of no benefit to my client, I will recommend settlement. Thus, the recommendation will have the direct effect of lowering my potential economic gain for the benefit of the client.

When I am defending a case and billing by the hour, I'm reminded of a quote by Thomas Jefferson. In the early 19th century, America was battling the Barbary Coast pirates off of North Africa. These pirates would frequently take American sailors hostage and hold them for ransom. Finally, growing exhausted by this practice, President Thomas Jefferson was quoted as saying, "Millions for defense, not one cent in tribute."

What was appropriate for dealing with Barbary Coast pirates back then may not always be in the best interests of my clients. Though "millions for defense, not one cent in tribute" is certainly of benefit to me as an attorney, I am obligated to place the best interests of my clients above my own.

Attorneys aren't the only ones who hold this legally defined obligation or duty. There are numerous professions who owe a fiduciary duty to others —the trustee of a trust or charitable foundation, stockbrokers, bankers, real estate agents, and even clergy owe a fiduciary duty to others. It is in this fiduciary relationship where a person agrees to place the best interests of others ahead of one's own. In a broad sense, anytime we have a potential to hold power over another, we theoretically create a fiduciary relationship. Essentially, we all have fiduciary obligations in most areas of our life regardless of profession.

Each fiduciary has specific duties depending on his or her role. These duties are subject to change if the fiduciary's relationship changes; however, the principle duty that always stays the same is that fiduciaries must always act in the best interest of somebody else, not themselves. The concept of a fiduciary is not new and has seen expanded application over time.

You may not agree with the full text of the original Hippocratic Oath, but it does demonstrate the age and origins of the fiduciary concept.

Original Hippocratic Oath of Doctors
The Hippocratic Oath
Original, translated from Greek.
"I swear by Aesculapius, Hygeia, and Panacea, and I take to witness all the gods, all the goddesses, to keep according to my ability and my judgment, the following Oath.

To consider dear to me as my parents him who taught me this art; to live in common with him and if necessary to share my goods with him; To look upon his children as my own brothers, to teach them this art if they so desire without fee or written promise; to impart to my sons and the sons of the master who taught me and the disciples who have enrolled themselves and have agreed to the rules of the profession, but to these alone the precepts and the instruction.

I will prescribe regimens for the good of my patients according to my ability and my judgment and never do harm to anyone.

To please no one will I prescribe a deadly drug nor give advice which may cause his death.

Nor will I give a woman a pessary to procure abortion.

But I will preserve the purity of my life and my arts.

I will not cut for stone, even for patients in whom the disease is manifest; I will leave this operation to be performed by practitioners, specialists in this art.

In every house where I come I will enter only for the good of my patients, keeping myself far from all intentional ill-doing and all seduction and especially from the pleasures of love with women or with men, be they free or slaves.

All that may come to my knowledge in the exercise of my profession or in daily commerce with men, which ought not to be spread abroad, I will keep secret and will never reveal.

If I keep this oath faithfully, may I enjoy my life and practice my art, respected by all men and in all times; but if I swerve from it or violate it, may the reverse be my lot."

I recently read an article by Tim Hammond entitled, "The Stolen Generation - Finding a Fiduciary Duty." In his article for the Murdoch University Electronic Journal of Law, Hammond described the early source of the fiduciary relationship:

The fiduciary relationship emerged from the Courts of Chancery in the earlier centuries. The primary aim of this equitable doctrine is to prevent those holding positions of power from abusing their authority.

The basic underlying purpose of the fiduciary obligation is to keep people honest and trustworthy — to keep them true to their role and to prevent them from abusing their power. The fiduciary rules have developed not because we are untrustworthy, but it is more a measure of ensuring that we exercise our duties without regard for personal gain, notoriety, or recognition. When we represent or make decisions on behalf of another person or organization, our priority is to consider only how it will affect them, not ourselves.

In an effort to ensure that a fiduciary performs his or her role in an ethical and coherent manner, the law has imposed upon him or her three specific and primary duties. The duties are **Obedience**, **Loyalty**, and **Care**. I strongly believe that if we exercise these duties in all aspects of our lives, we can get what we want <u>without</u> getting in trouble.

Chapter Eight

THE THREE DUTIES OF THE FIDUCARY

Obedience

Obedience is the first duty. Many would assume that obedience simply means to obey or to be submissive. It does not always. In terms of the fiduciary obligation, obedience simply means honor —to honor what you are obligated to do, what you say you will do, and then to be honest by telling the truth about how you did it.

> **Obedience**: The duty requires a fiduciary to act in accordance with agreed to contracts, governing documents as well as all applicable laws and regulations.

A good example of obedience is taking an oath. Many positions of authority and trust are required to swear to an oath. For example, the President of the United States must swear to protect and defend the Constitution of the United States. This is not only an expression of loyalty but specific outward expression of obedience to a governing document or principle.

> *"I do solemnly swear (or affirm) that I will faithfully execute the office of President of the United States, and will to the best of my ability, preserve, protect, and defend the Constitution of the United States."*
> - Copyright 2002 by CB Presidential Research Services

Loyalty

The second duty of a fiduciary is Loyalty. Loyalty means taking Obedience to the next level. Loyalty is doing what you say you'll do even if there's nothing in it for you; in fact, loyalty expects you to advance the interests of another. The duty of loyalty goes one step further by requiring that we carry out our responsibilities and promises even if it means we must make personal or financial sacrifices. In other words, to be loyal you should do what you said you would do—even if it costs you.

> **Loyalty**: Being steadfast in allegiance to a person, ideal or custom.

An excellent example of loyalty is that of former NFL Player, Pat Tillman. Tillman deferred a $3.6 million contract as a Safety with the Arizona Cardinals to join the military after the September 11th attacks. Tillman was killed April 22, 2004, while serving as an Army Ranger on a mission in Southeastern Afghanistan. Clearly, Pat Tillman's actions demonstrated a "steadfast allegiance" to an entity, ideal, or custom. Tillman was not drafted or forced into service but joined the military out of a sense of duty. His service was the fulfillment of an obligation to others, which resulted in his paying the ultimate price. Pat Tillman is but one example among many who have across generations sacrificed everything for their sense of duty to the United States.

Care

Care is the third, but by no means the least important, duty of a fiduciary. The common usage of "care" can mean "mental distress, concern, or grief." While a fiduciary can certainly experience grief or distress, that's not what is meant here. Applied to a fiduciary, care means that a person must use the care (i.e. concern) an ordinarily prudent person would use under the same or similar circumstances.

> **Care**: Using the concern an ordinarily prudent person would use under the same or similar circumstances.

This so-called prudent person or "prudent man rule" basically comes down to the fact that we should employ common sense and good judgment.

Excerpts from "The Prudence of Abraham Lincoln" by Allen C. Guelzo.

The most obvious example of Lincoln's prudence at work is his handling of slavery and emancipation. It has become common—and was common in Lincoln's own day among the abolitionists—to denounce Lincoln as "an equivocating, vacillating leader," to borrow the words of W.E.B. DuBois. Lincoln's chief aim was "the integrity of the Union and not the emancipation of the slaves; that if he could keep the Union from being disrupted, he would not only allow slavery to exist but would loyally protect it." But consider what Lincoln's options for emancipation really were. In an era before the Fourteenth Amendment, civil rights (including the definition of citizenship) were state prerogatives, protected from federal review.

Much as he "was himself opposed to slavery," Lincoln could not "see how the abolitionists could reach it in the slave states." Demands for immediate abolition might satisfy some Romantic yearning for justice over law, but as long as slavery was a state institution, any attempt to emancipate slaves by executive order would be at once challenged by the states in the federal courts—and the federal judiciary, all the way up to the Supreme Court, had shown itself repeatedly and profoundly hostile to the idea. Abolitionists, Lincoln complained, "seemed to think that the moment I was president, I had the power to abolish slavery, forgetting that before I could have any power whatsoever I had to take the oath to support the Constitution of the United States as I found them."

On the other hand, immediate abolition was not the only avenue to emancipation. The federal government might have no direct power to interfere in state matters, but it did have considerable fiscal powers with which it could tempt slave states to abandon slavery by legislative action and embrace a federally funded buy-out. And within six months of his inauguration, Lincoln had initiated a campaign for legislative emancipation, beginning with Delaware, the weakest of the four slave states that remained loyal to the Union. This legislative option was based "upon these conditions: First, that the abolition should be gradual. Second, that it should be on a vote of the majority of the qualified voters of the District; and third that compensation should be made to unwilling owners." Handled this way, emancipation would set up what he expected would be a domino-effect among the slave states for emancipation.

Unhappily for Lincoln, the loyal slave states threw his offer back in his face. So, in the summer of 1862, he turned instead to a military order that freed the Confederacy's slaves—what we now know as the Emancipation Proclamation. But because the proclamation was only a military order, prudence dictated that he limit its application to those slave states in actual rebellion against the Union. And since little (if any) legal precedent existed for the use of presidential "war powers" in this way, he continued to back a legislative strategy, parallel to his war-powers proclamation, and in the end, it was that legislative strategy that produced black freedom in the Thirteenth Amendment. Between these two strategies, legislative and military, Lincoln saw no conflict. He told federal judge Thomas Duval that "he saw nothing

inconsistent with the gradual emancipation of slavery and his proclamation."
Lincoln's procedure was at every step a model of prudence.

The duty of care appears to be the simplest, but, in fact, can prove to be the most demanding of all the duties. Most people exercise care in many areas of their life without ever knowing it. For example, a prudent police officer will interview all known witnesses to a crime before preparing a report. Common sense and good judgment dictate thoroughness and diligence in investigating a crime. Another example comes from the previously mentioned oath of the President which states "and will to the best of my ability." This is essentially the duty of care: an agreement to do the best of your ability. This duty does not demand perfection. But rather, doing the best you can do which often requires that you ask for help when needed.

Fiduciary duties are so important that the law specifically requires that some professions exercise the duties of obedience, loyalty, and care. Their creation and evolution have occurred over a great deal of time and for good reason. Each duty depends upon the other and the exercise of each duty independently and in unison with the others insures we remain thoughtful and deliberate in decision making. In the following chapters, we will discuss the application of each in greater detail. And, as you have probably surmised, we will apply these fiduciary duties to explaining our ethical dilemma involving the Juvenile Judge.

Chapter Nine

THE OBEDIENT FIDUCIARY

I truly believe one reason we don't always do what we agree to do is because we simply don't have the time. All too often, it becomes difficult to do the things we say we will do, not because we don't want to, but because we agree to do too much. It seems that people have so much on their plate these days that it's all they can do to juggle back and forth between them. It seems as if there just aren't enough hours in the day to devote a heightened level of diligence, attention, and focus to any one particular thing.

Being overcommitted and overextended does not excuse us from doing the things we agreed to do. In fact, honoring our word is so essential in personal, as well as professional relationships, that the law has made honoring our word a duty of the fiduciary. That duty is called Obedience.

As an attorney, I have taken an oath that I would always honor the truth. As an officer of the court, I must not allow anyone to commit perjury. In other words, if I know the truth and am aware that someone is being dishonest, I am obligated to inform the court. The idea behind this code of conduct, as an attorney is that I am a fiduciary not only for my client but also to the entire legal system. I owe a heightened or special responsibility to the truth. Still, I must admit there are times when it is difficult for attorneys, including myself, to be obedient and honor their word, because their duty to the court can conflict with their duty to their client. Many attorneys have encountered situations where their client was not being honest to the court. Granted, dishonesty or evasion of the truth can be advantageous to the client, and sometimes, this dishonesty doesn't harm the other side. However, a lie is still a lie. I am obligated to represent and exercise a heightened level of obligation to honesty in the search for justice.

Attorneys are not the only ones who have an obligation to be obedient and honor their roles. For example, a real estate agent also has a duty of obedience. The governing document with a real estate agent is a listing agreement or buyer representation agreement. This transaction of home and property happens hundreds if not thousands of times a day. The agent's duty of obedience is to honor the terms and conditions of the contract as promptly and as efficiently as possible and effect all lawful instructions from his or her client.

While I use lawyers and real estate agents as contemporary examples, we all have an obligation to be obedient in the roles we undertake. As you read this, you have likely identified similar situations in your life.

My colleague and contributing author, John Glover, and I are intrigued by history. There is an interesting series of events involving Deadwood, South Dakota that eventually led to a U.S. Supreme Court decision in 1883. The facts of the case demonstrate a fine example of obedience or honoring one's word.

A conflict arose between two Tribal members residing on the Rosebud Sioux Reservation resulting in the death of one, Spotted Tail, a highly revered leader. By traditional means, his assailant, Crow Dog, was held accountable by the Tribe and required to provide restitution to Spotted Tail's family. Much to the consternation of the newly arrived settlers in Dakota Territory, Crow Dog was not executed for his actions. This eventually prompted the white authorities to arrest and incarcerate Crow Dog in the Deadwood jail while court proceedings were initiated.

Crow Dog cooperated with these authorities but insisted that he must meet his obligations to Spotted Tail's family. On his honor, Crow Dog was permitted to leave his Deadwood confinement under the condition he return. Now I do not know about you, but I believe many of us would overlook our commitment to return to jail and escape a foreign government's culturally and morally different expectations of justice. Nonetheless, Crow Dog did return to face uncertain and likely deadly consequences in obedience, or in honor, of his personal commitment.

Interestingly, the U.S. Supreme Court found that the Territorial authorities lacked jurisdiction over a criminal matter between two Native Americans occurring on a Reservation and Crow Dog was released.[2]

What is striking, however, is Crow Dog's exceptional example of obedience as it related to honoring his word. His commitment to meeting his obligation compelled him to take a personal oath of submission to the will of these foreign authorities, a submission that would at the time likely lead to an "unjust" consequence by his own culture's standards. Nonetheless, he honored his word, not only with regard to his tribal obligations but also to the white authorities—again, a fine example of obedience expected of a true fiduciary. I believe that it is also particularly important to note that Crow Dog not only honored his word but managed to act in accordance with agreed to contracts, governing documents as well as all applicable laws and regulations in two distinct cultures.

Obedience is doing what we said we would do. To be obedient means that if we made a promise or an agreement, we will keep it. Obedience is a politician who delivers on campaign promises. Obedience is getting the report finished on time or presenting an offer to purchase to a client regardless of the amount. Obedience is even reporting to work on time. These are all examples of honoring what we said we would do, whether it is a specific promise or one that is implied.

Permeating the duty of obedience are notions of respect. People should not only do what they agree to do, but they should respect others, too. The duty of obedience in daily life is less dramatic than Crow Dog's situation. When we accept a job or take a class, we agree to do certain things. If we don't show up on time for work or for class, it is disruptive and disrespectful. It's one thing to be disrespectful to ourselves, but it's an entirely different issue when we are unfair and inconsiderate to others. Obedience encompasses a basic form of civility and respect for others. Obviously, Crow Dog looked at honor and respect for others at its highest level.

People who consistently promise but do not deliver do not get ahead. They may obtain limited short term success but it is most often fleeting. I was initially impressed as I saw Andrew Fastow, Chief Financial Officer of Enron, and Jeff Skilling, President of Enron, rise well above middle management, but I also watched each walk out of the federal courthouse in Houston in handcuffs.

The world is full of extraordinarily talented people who fail to appreciate the idea of honoring their obligations and doing what they say they will do. People who honor their obligations and are obedient to their word are the best friends, partners, and performers. It is the exceptional people who consistently demonstrate this idea of honor. We aspire to be like them.

How do we apply the duty of Obedience? The initial step in developing a protocol to successfully implement this duty is to ask yourself the following questions in the midst of any dilemma or difficult circumstance:

1.   *"What did I agree to do?"*

This agreement could be an oath, a written contract, or the acceptance of a job which requires certain skills. Now it is not enough to simply review signed documents and job descriptions. The duty of obedience requires even more. Even in this era of technology and contractual requirements, the verbal word remains powerful.

2.   *"What did I say I would do?"*

Obviously, if we said we would do it, then obedience means we honor our word. We are not done yet. Frequently communication whether verbal or written can be misunderstood or misconstrued. The duty of obedience requires we honor the beliefs and expectations associated with our agreement as well.

3.   *"What are the understood expectations of this agreement for me?"*

This sounds a bit more complicated than it really is in practice. For example, if your child asks, "can you pick me up at school today" and your response is "Yes," what is the understanding? For me, the understanding is the child wishes to be picked up when school is dismissed, not at 9:00 p.m. tonight. This same principle holds true in business as well. What is the expectation of the agreement? Obviously, this requires you to be honest with yourself.

4.   *"Is this agreement legal?"*

The fundamental goal of a fiduciary is to act in the best interest of another. Inevitably, this means making decisions on behalf of someone else which has legal significance. As we mentioned earlier, the fiduciaries of Enron, MCI/WorldCom and others made decisions of legal consequence which were not proper under all applicable laws, regulations and governing documents. Clearly, these unlawful and inappropriate acts by the fiduciary did not benefit others. With the duty of obedience, a fiduciaries actions and decisions must be lawful otherwise they cannot be ethical.

This duty of obedience is not only legal, it is truly a human expectation as well. In our dilemma, the Judge's expectations are that the Reporter will honor the terms of the contract even though the Judge was not forthright about his guilt before the signing of this contract. Our reporter agreed to honor the contract, but did very little beforehand to discover the implications of his agreement. Years ago, our word accompanied by a simple handshake was a legal and binding contract. Our word was not taken lightly. Agreements we made as people were the basis for our interaction and economy. This is why such agreements should not be made in haste nor should the agreement violate the law.

If we embrace this concept, our life gets easier—not more difficult. The first step of ethical and effective decision making starts, as it should, with a strong foundation in the fiduciary's duty of obedience.

Chapter Ten

THE LOYAL FIDUCIARY

Obedience means honoring our word, but loyalty is the ingredient that helps others to know that we will, indeed, honor our word. Think of it as a feeling of attachment to something or someone that takes precedence over our own interests. Loyalty is doing what we said we would do even when there is nothing in it for us, or in fact, it might work to our detriment.

Loyalty changes our priorities, steering them away from ourselves to other people or causes. Whether we're at work or play, it means that we should consider how our actions or decisions affect someone else's best interests rather than our own.

In my mind, loyalty takes obedience to the next level. You do what you said you would do even if there is no gain, reward, or compensation to you —even if adhering to those principles costs you.

Loyalty is not all about sacrifice, however; it does have its rewards. The standard of loyalty in business produces long-term employees and a lower turnover rate. There is considerable expense involved in training new employees, and during that training process, productivity is lower. Increasingly, employees, vendors, and clients seek to create a relationship. This relationship is premised upon the duty of loyalty. The creation of loyalty is facilitated by an environment which provides a sense of security and shared ethical decision making.

A Hudson Institute survey found that "employees who believe they work in an ethical environment are six times more likely to be loyal then workers who believe their company is unethical."

Employees can be loyal to their employers, and vice versa. Often, the greatest impact of loyalty is felt when a company is loyal to its employees. One of the best examples of this practice is the true story of Aaron Feuerstein. Mr. Feuerstein, now retired, was the owner of a Massachusetts company called Malden Mills. In 1995, his factory burned to the ground. Mr. Feuerstein decided to rebuild his plant in the same small community where it had originated rather than opening a more economical overseas site. What is more striking is that he also took the amazing and unprecedented step of continuing to provide full pay and benefits to the thousands of Malden Mills employees during the idle months while the factory was being rebuilt. I can imagine that some people would consider this to be a terrible business decision.

In an article in <u>Parade</u> magazine dated September 8, 1996, Feuerstein was quoted as saying:

> *"I have a responsibility to the worker, both blue-collar and white-collar. I have an equal responsibility to the community. It would have been unconscionable to put 3,000 people on the streets and deliver a deathblow to the cities of Lawrence and Methuen. Maybe on paper our company is worthless to Wall Street, but I can tell you it's worth more."*

What did Aaron Feuerstein and Malden Mills get for their loyalty? For one thing, the company held an impressive 95 percent employee retention rate. Employee production also skyrocketed after the factory was rebuilt. The fact that over 3,000 people were grateful and loyal to their employer is reflected as Feuerstein said, "Before the fire, that plant produced 130,000 yards a week. A few weeks after reopening, it was up to 230,000 yards. Our people became very creative. They were willing to work 25 hours a day."

The Malden Mills story is a compelling one. It is about a business that is vested in its employees and the community. The company had suffered setbacks, including bankruptcy, in the past. Yet, it performed an act of loyalty that was above and beyond all expectations. This story depicts how loyalty eventually benefits all parties, even if it requires sacrifice and expense.

Loyalty extends beyond clients, customers, or expectations of employers and employees. Dedication and trust impact all walks of life. Loyalty represents a strong feeling of attachment to a particular person, company, or cause. It is not artificial, selfish, or self-absorbed.

There are events and experiences in all of our lives that challenge our sense of loyalty. This challenge is often a function of financial pressures in our lives. It has been my observation that people are at their best when they are a part of something that is not all about them. This sense of belonging eases the fear brought with financial and emotional insecurity.

U.S. Automakers Could Take Lesson in Loyalty from Toyota
By Larry Ingraham
Indianapolis Star—March 20, 2006
The end of 2005 brought Hoosiers good news from Japan, as Toyota unveiled an innovative plan to build thousands of cars at the Subaru plant in Lafayette. This will be Toyota's second auto-production site in Indiana (along with Princeton), making Indiana the only state in the U.S. where Toyota will produce vehicles in two locations.
Toyota's decision tells us a lot about what the company values: hard work, honest partners and loyalty.
I caught an up-close glimpse of how important loyalty is to the Toyota leadership in October 2003 during a three-day business conference in Osaka, Japan.
A keynote speaker one of the days was Fujio Cho, then president of Toyota Motor Corp. His presentation focused on Toyota's strong sales trend that year in the U.S. market. Afterward, other Japanese and American audience members and I rushed up to the front to introduce ourselves.
When my turn came, I exchanged business cards with him and told him three things as he held my card formally in both of his hands: I told him I was from Indiana, I thanked him for helping to open a Toyota plant in Princeton and mentioned that my family owned three Toyota vehicles.
Upon hearing this last point, Cho bowed deeply three times repeating, "Thank you very much!" in English.
There were several junior staff members from Toyota who were hovering close by. I could sense that they and the long line of greeters behind me were quite surprised by the CEO's actions. Doubtless, two things crossed their minds: Who is this fat, white guy? and what did he say to make the president of one of the worlds most powerful and influential companies formally bow to him three times?
I was just as surprised and flattered by Coho's gesture.
Since this experience, I often wonder how the presidents of GM or Ford would have responded if I had told them I owned three of their cars. I can guess that they would have said something like, "Please buy more!" But I doubt they would have taken my hand in both of theirs and shaken it warmly, and professed sincere thanks to me —the customer.

That same sense of loyalty extends into all aspects of our lives. It is a calculated and rational behavior which is instilled and inherent in our being. Without a sense of loyalty, it would be easy to walk away from people, employers, and causes. When loyalty is a factor, however, the risks of exiting become greater because we have a personal stake. The application of the duty of loyalty does not have to be as dramatic as that of Mr. Feuerstein or Pat Tillman. However, it is critical in making an effective ethical decision.

Following up on our previous questions involving Obedience, we now turn to the second phase of the protocol. The Loyalty principle in successful ethical decision making is determined by the answers to these questions.

1. *"Who is Involved?"*

Simply identify or make a list of the persons affected by your decision and the potential consequences to each. During this analysis be mindful of the duty of obedience or what we agreed to do. Further, you are likely one of the persons involved. It is important, however, to resist the temptation to focus on yourself.

2. *"Of those involved, what is my obligation to each?"*

This phase of decision making is intended to focus us on our sense of loyalty toward others. It is like the behavior Mr. Feuerstein demonstrated toward his employees and community. The Reporter in our dilemma faces conflicting obligations and must choose to whom he owes a fiduciary duty.

As for any personal concerns, just relax. The decision which most benefits others will ultimately benefit you as well. Perhaps the greatest gift of loyalty is what it gives us as individuals, the quiet sense of having done the right thing and the security of being a part of something greater than ourselves. Further, loyalty generally has the consequence of meaningful future benefits as we saw in Mr. Feuerstein's experience.

Chapter Eleven

THE CAREFUL FIDUCIARY

Most would ultimately agree that the happiest and most successful people are the ones who are actively engaged in their lives, rather than those whose lives actively engage them. They know what needs to be accomplished and how to go about achieving it. They are the ones who reap personal satisfaction and rewards from a job well done. These people know how to apply the standard of a fiduciary's care in their own lives.

> **Care**: "means that degree of care that would be used by a person of ordinary prudence under the same or similar circumstances."
> -Texas Pattern Jury Charge 2003 Edition

In the language of the law, the fiduciary duty of care is essentially the "prudent person" or "prudent man" rule, i.e., common sense and good judgment. It requires us to be diligent, timely, and active in our agreed upon responsibilities.

As I think about the duty of care, it is my opinion that there is clearly a relationship between prudence and time. An ordinary prudent person does not act in haste or in an impulsive manner. Rather, he or she will TAKE THE TIME to make a thoughtful decision. Thus, I would argue that central to making an ethical decision is taking the time, or making the time, to thoughtfully deliberate before deciding.

> **Deliberate**: *intransitive verb*: to think about or discuss issues and decisions carefully; *transitive verb*: to think about <u>deliberately</u> and often with formal discussion before reaching a decision
> Merriam-Webster's Online Dictionary www.m-w.com

It is important to point out that exercising the duty of care will not always result in the absolute correct answer, but on the whole it demonstrates that the decision maker has approached this duty with the appropriate vigor and diligence. Stated another way, being a good fiduciary does not mean that you will always be right, but in relation to the duty of care, it means that you have taken the time to allow the best possible result. We cannot control all things. Ultimately, it is out of our hands but as the Arab proverb says in times of a desert storm, "trust in Allah but tie your camel," meaning that we should make necessary preparations for an optimal result.

If you will recall, earlier we mentioned the impact of time on ethical decision making, the time for deliberation and thoughtful consideration of a decision or dilemma. This is essential to honoring the duty of care. It is prudence which dictates that we take the time to do the best we can do.

Care is about exercising good judgment and common sense in our decisions and actions. It is about knowing our abilities, as well as our weaknesses, and using that knowledge when we make decisions or actions that affect not only ourselves, but others.

Care is your own personal, fail-safe system in decision making. It's a checks and balance system that keeps our lives on an even keel. Think about what happens when we become overcommitted, stressed, or get in too far over our heads. We scramble to complete our work, often taking shortcuts or making mistakes which could have broad consequences. Placing ourselves in this position is unfortunate, and, in my opinion, unnecessary.

"Americans will spend an estimated $14 billion fighting stress next year according to market data." MSNBC.com Health editor. Linda Dahlstrom, November 30, 2006

The ability to make a successful ethical decision can be seriously jeopardized when we do not have the time or focus to make a considered decision. The foundation for exercising good judgment is being prudent and aware of our own limitations, especially the limitations on our time.

Prudent: Latin term marked by wisdom or judiciousness; shrewd in the management of practical affairs and marked by circumspection. - *Merriam-Webster Online dictionary www.m-w.com (2006)*

As I've said, Care is exercising good judgment and doing what a normally prudent person would do under similar circumstances.

But, how are we to know what a normally prudent person would do? How do we know that we are indeed exercising good judgment? By asking and honestly answering the following three simple questions, I believe that we can be certain we are applying the principle of care.

Following up on our previous questions involving obedience and loyalty, we now turn to the third phase of the protocol for successful ethical decision making. The Care principle is determined by the answers to these questions.

1. *"What is in the best interest of the persons for whom I am making the decision?"*

In fact, best interest can mean many things. For example, what is in the best interest of a child's education may conflict with what is in the best interest of a child's health. A great school in Minnesota is not such a great idea for a child who is predisposed to bronchitis or pneumonia.

Within this question is another. Does it make sense that I would decide this issue at this time? Time is a critical component with multiple applications. Time is not only a measure of being thoughtful and unrushed, but it is also a function of good judgment. Time can also mean timing. There are those circumstances when not making the decision at that moment is the best interim step.

For example, a head football coach in a playoff game may face a fourth down and fifteen yards to go on his own thirty yard line, in a tie game with ten seconds to play. Prudence may dictate doing nothing but running out the clock to avoid a costly mistake and allow the game to be decided in overtime. The same can be said for some decisions. There are those instances when the best decision is to wait until the playing field is more favorable for success.

Complicating matters is the reality that we simply do not know the answer. Unfortunately, this does not relieve a fiduciary of the duty of care and the need for a decision. This leads us to the next consideration:

2. *"Am I in a position to decide this on my own?"*

Most of us are familiar with the title of general contractor in construction; however, few of us are truly sure of what that individual does. As I understand it, the general contractor finds, organizes, and directs all aspects of the project and his or her decision is final. However, a general contractor may not be an electrician, carpenter, or a plumber. These trades require special knowledge and training. This leads us to the third question.

3. *"Where do I find the answer?"*

The general contractor typically defers to the judgment of the electrician as to how to properly wire the house for power, even though it is the general contractor who is ultimately responsible for the whole project.

We see this in numerous professions. The medical profession has multiple specialties including cardiology, internist, general surgeons, neurosurgeons, etc. If a general practitioner does not know some important information about how to handle a patient's case, he or she asks someone to help find it. In other words, he or she sends you to a specialist.

The same concepts can apply to any person facing a difficult decision which can significantly affect others. We all frequently face a time when we need advice from others with more knowledge, skill, and training than we may have. Acknowledging that we may need the guidance and knowledge of others is essential to successful ethical decision making.

Ultimately, all decisions for which we are responsible are up to us. The key here is that we have made every effort to obtain the information and seek the advice of those who can provide useful knowledge and insight. In the end, the decision will be up to our own common sense and good judgment.

"To thine own self be true." Polonius to son Laertes
- *Hamlet, Act I Scene iii, William Shakespeare*

Let's be clear about this concept. Just because we don't know the answer doesn't mean that we are not capable of doing the job and doing it well. It simply means that we know we need further information and resources in order to act with the standard of care that is required. This is especially true when you hold positions of leadership. I have rarely, if ever, met a leader in any capacity who was the smartest person in the room. But, every good leader I have met surrounded himself or herself with smart people and listened. This brings us to the next area of inquiry.

4. *"Do I have the authority to make this decision?"*

This question is central to my actions as an attorney. Regardless of circumstances, I cannot settle a case without my client's consent. For example, being hired as an attorney by a client allows me considerable leeway but it does not grant me complete control. Ultimately, the decision to go to trial or settle a case is that of my client. The same is true with the Real Estate Broker. The Broker cannot unilaterally reduce the price of a seller's home or accept an offer from a buyer without consent from the client.

The same is true in medical care. For example, the patient ultimately decides whether or not to have surgery. In most circumstances, a doctor does not have the legal or moral authority to make that decision.

Issues of authority arise everyday in every profession. It is highly unlikely that a car salesman will cut the price of a vehicle to close a sale without approval from a supervisor. Unfortunately, decisions are made each day without authority. The result of unilateral and unauthorized decisions always results in conflict and frequently creates disastrous results. Imagine the potential results if our Reporter decides to make a decision without the benefit of others' advice.

No decision is in anyone's best interest if we do not have the authority to make this decision. Only the President has the authority to order military action on behalf of the United States. If each governor or U.S. Senator had such authority, there would be chaos. Before any decision we must confirm it is our decision to make.

Chapter Twelve

"YES, I CARE"..."NO, I CAN'T"

The principle of care is essentially remaining true to the overriding duty to act for someone else while being conscientious of all other factors. Care is focused attention, taking notice, and being conscious of particulars.

Care: Old English term meaning painstaking or watchful attention.
- Merriam Webster's Online Dictionary, www.m-w.com (2006)

I don't know about you, but I'm not good at details. As a matter of fact, details drive me crazy. When I am particularly busy, details are my own ultimate nemesis. Patience and focus are areas in which I need considerable improvement. I'll be the first to admit that I have a limited attention span, so I make sure I have people on my staff that are good with details and organization. The key point here is not to focus on just our weak points, because it is our strengths that make us who we are. However, we need to recognize when we might not be equipped to make a decision, and to get help; being willing to do that is an admirable quality in itself.

The questions recommended earlier are just a start, a basic foundation for operating a process of good judgment. You have likely noticed that notions of time and timing permeate the description of the duty of care. Frankly, our meeting the required care obligation demands recognition of time constraints. Care further demands a conscious effort to take or make the time necessary for decision making.

There are different aspects of time to be considered. For example, it is wise never to try to take on everything. When we do, we become overburdened. Unfortunately, that is easier said than done. To be quite honest, I find myself constantly taking on more responsibility when I barely have time for what I have now. No matter how we look at the clock, there are only so many hours in a day. Time is one of the biggest constraints that limit our ability to fulfill our duties with the proper degree of care.

Overburdening usually leads to greater disorganization, further hampering productivity. Thought processes can become short-circuited when overloaded and memories fail; correspondingly, we also fail to meet our obligations. All this jeopardizes our ability to make successful ethical decisions.

A 2003 survey conducted by the Ethics Resource Center and the Society for Human Resource Management found that "meeting overly aggressive business objective" was cited by 48 percent of respondents as the leading cause of pressure to compromise standards.

Hopefully, prior to becoming overloaded, we accept the fact that we need to delegate some of our responsibilities to other capable people. This doesn't relieve us of the responsibility, just the task.

The very time constraints that require delegating occasionally require that we learn to say "no." "No, I'm sorry; right now I have too many other obligations to give that task the proper amount of attention and care it deserves." For most of us, this is truly difficult. We often feel compelled to participate for reasons quite altruistic and for economic reasons. Saying "yes" when we should say "no" can lead not only to compromising standards but to a miserable existence.

Critical to success at this stage is being honest to oneself. Taking on too much can turn an opportunity into a career albatross.

While care is important to the fiduciary's obligations, transferring the concept of care to ethical living can be challenging. In this context, time takes on yet another meaning. Whether we are at work or at home with our family, care requires that we be present and mentally active in the moment. Our lives can be cluttered and scattered with appointments, to-do lists, expectations, and obligations. Though increasingly difficult, our presence of mind is critical to this duty.

Here again this is always easier said than done. Sometimes we don't even have control over our tasks, as is evidenced by an Ethics Resource Center (ERC) and Society for Human Resource Management (SHRM) survey. It stated that the second leading cause of pressure to result in the compromise of ethical standards is the "need to follow bosses' directives." Loosely translated, we are given far too much to do to in a limited amount of time.

Here, we arrive at an all too familiar scenario. In an economic culture of hyper-competitiveness and financial insecurity, we struggle to say "no" to our boss or supervisor. Indeed, this is a true dilemma.

That's exactly why we should pause and take a minute to ask ourselves the questions I posed earlier. If we base our decisions and actions on our honest answers, we can keep our lives in balance. Only then can we really be able to fully participate in the present — to be mindful of the task at hand, and to gently, not frantically, move on to the next.

All of us will likely face a time when an honest answer may mean saying "no" or disagreeing with those in positions of authority. Integrity is the complete and incorruptible adherence to principle. This is when our loyalty to care or integrity comes into play. My personal definition of integrity is as follows:

Integrity is doing the right thing, even when you are afraid.

Saying "no" or "I will need help" even if you are in fear, will likely be of more long term benefit to your career than saying "yes" and risking a poor performance. If we apply the protocol of successful ethical decision making, the answer, no matter how difficult, will likely be in the best interest of everyone concerned.

Chapter Thirteen

ETHICAL DECISION MAKING AND SUCCESS

Having examined the duties of a fiduciary you might be wondering, "Can a person actually succeed in this day and age consistently doing what is ethically expected?" I would emphatically reply, "True success can only be achieved by consistent ethical decision making!" I believe this to be true whatever your particular definition of success may be. The evidence is clearly apparent in our recent history.

Take business practices, for example. We are all too aware of the cost of unethical behavior, ranging from bankruptcies to declining stock value, customer distrust, indictments, and insider trading, as well as loss of income, reputation, and trust. The compelling question is if the consequences of such behavior and actions are so severe, why would we continue to engage in such behavior?

I think part of the answer to that question is based on individual circumstances. Employees might engage in a particular behavior because their employer also does —and that same employer is the one who evaluates, pays and promotes them. Therefore, it would seem fitting that they would base their behavior on their employer's.

Other reasons for questionable, or even criminal ethics in the business world are due to underlying pressures to perform. These pressures all too often don't allow us the opportunity to make long term decisions —shortcuts become necessary. In the "faster is better" society that we live in, there is a perception that being slow or being second can mean the death of a career, an idea, or a company.

We live in a society that commonly uses terms like "the ends justify the means," or "just make it happen," insinuating that we believe that it's acceptable under certain circumstances to be dishonest or unethical if it gets us what we want. Moreover, there are some who believe that our actions and behavior are not wrong unless we get caught. Our jails and prisons are full of such people (who may not be sorry for their crimes, but are sorry that they weren't smarter about how they did it).

These philosophies are morally and ethically wrong. But more to the immediate point, such philosophies are inaccurate and unprofitable. Countless convicted CEOs, directors, accountants, financial investors, bankers, politicians, teachers, athletes, and even church leaders would likely agree.

The Ethics Resource Center (ERC), an organization located in Washington, D.C., is dedicated to the promotion of ethical conduct by businesses and corporations in the United States. The ERC represents those companies who are dedicated to doing the right thing and who have a written commitment to social responsibility. More importantly, they act on that commitment. In other words, they not only talk the talk, they walk the walk.

The ERC also provides data which demonstrates that companies which are committed to social responsibility consistently are more profitable than those who aren't. For example, James Burke, Chairman of Johnson and Johnson, said "If you invested $30,000 in a composite Dow Jones 30 years ago, it would be worth $134,000 today. However, if you took that same $30,000 and divided it 15 ways ($2,000 each), and invested those funds into 15 socially and ethically responsible firms, it would now be worth $1,061,800!" The Ethics Index tracks the stock performance of publicly traded organizations which have been recognized for their superior corporate citizenship, ability to attract and retain employees, and sustainability practices. Ethics Index companies have outperformed the Standard and Poor's 500 by nearly 400 percent over the past five years.[3]

Evidence strongly shows that those companies and people committed to ethical and responsible practices are profitable and successful. Each demonstrates by practice and example that incorporating the interest of others is not only the right thing to do but profitable as well.

It doesn't matter who we are or what title we hold, I believe that we all can get what we want without getting in trouble. In fact, it is the only way to keep what we want once it is obtained. The reality is that those who participate in unethical behavior almost always get caught. It is just a matter of time.

How is ethical business success to be achieved? In his article "Ethical Leadership: The State of the Art," Herb Rubenstein stated that "ethical leadership should be a process designed on what to do, not on what not to do." In effect, Rubenstein is simply stating that leaders best promote ethics in the workplace when they teach and exercise appropriate behavior. Standing in front of a group of employees and telling them what is unacceptable is not enough; they must demonstrate and exercise acceptable behavior. The inherent role of a leader is to place the best interest of others above his or her own interest.

It is with this in mind that the duties of a fiduciary come into play. Clearly, they could be used to determine "what to do'" in our daily personal and professional life. And, by doing so, we demonstrate to others the ethical decision making process. We, in fact, walk the walk.

Companies who are responsible and accountable to their customers, employees, and communities earn respect, trust, and loyalty. They also enjoy the benefits of high employee retention, low turnover, and a reputation for honesty. They enjoy savings of substantial sums of money in training, as well as additional savings derived from not having to pay for the legal expenses associated with unethical behavior.

Even through adverse times, a company can benefit and actually profit from applying the duties of a fiduciary. Take into consideration the devastation that must have been felt by the makers of Tylenol products. In the autumn of 1982, someone placed potassium cyanide in random bottles of Extra Strength Tylenol capsules, causing the deaths of seven people in the Chicago area. Johnson & Johnson, the owners of McNeil Consumer Products, completely stopped production of the capsules, and pulled an estimated 30 million bottles of the product from shelves all over the nation. They also agreed to replace over 22 million bottles of the capsules which were already in consumers' homes. Johnson & Johnson went a step further and recalled all of their products, not just the capsules, in all regions across the country.

This was an extremely costly move for the manufacturer, which surely resulted in massive expense. However, it was the company's response that actually earned it a robust standing in the marketplace. Although company executives were being strongly advised to discontinue Tylenol products completely or at the very least to rename the product, they refused to do so. The makers of Tylenol believed in their product and had faith that the consumer would react favorably to their response. Within two months, Tylenol reemerged, having invented the tamper-proof seal which has now become mandatory for all over-the-counter drugs. This move eventually made Tylenol the most-trusted brand of pain reliever in the industry and produced long term customer loyalty. As noted in an October 31, 2005 article by The Associated Press and published by MSNBC.com, Tylenol has been on the market for more than 50 years and is in the medicine cabinets of 70 percent of American households even after the tampering scare 20 years ago. I think most would agree this extraordinary response demonstrated a corporation exercising the duty of care. It takes years to build customer trust, but as evidenced in this situation, trust can be lost in just one week. Even in adverse times, doing the right and socially responsible thing, regardless of the expense involved, proved to benefit Tylenol.

Another example of a corporation which recognized its fiduciary obligations is TEOCO. TEOCO is a company that has reaped the benefits of ethical behavior. The company is employee owned; its name is actually an acronym for "The Employee Owned Company." TEOCO provides telecom solutions products and telecom auditing services. It is the provider of BillTrak Pro, a data and invoice audit management software program which is used to audit over $12 billion of invoices in the telecom market every year.

TEOCO's leaders chose from the onset to stress ethics and values with its customers and employee-owners. They hold regular meetings to discuss ethics and issues that arise. Their core values scroll across their website (www.teoco.com), stressing Alignment with Employees, Clients, and Community. Here again, they not only talk the talk, but they walk the walk. They've established an Advisory Group to maintain a constant focus on their Fairfax, Virginia community and have made belief in their core values the first qualification for employment with their company.

During the first five years of its existence, TEOCO leaders reported a growth of an astronomical 1,873 percent, with revenues that grew from $346,000 to $6.8 million dollars during that time. They have since continued with consecutive growth every year since then.

As a small business, TEOCO was not required to develop an ethics program, but its founder, Atul Jain, would have it no other way. The program is a model ethics program for small businesses which is based on Jain's concept that a company and its employees do not have to "sell their soul in order to succeed." The results of the company's ethics program and community involvement and social responsibility proves that investing in doing the right thing in the right way is beneficial to any business, regardless of its size.

These companies are not isolated examples. The Business Ethics magazine, which is based in Minneapolis, Minnesota, names the Top 100 companies in its Annual Business Ethics Awards. Both large and small businesses are included. They are selected for their ethics program and their community involvement, and selection is based upon their accountability to their stakeholders, shareholders, community, and employees. The top award recipient is previously mentioned Green Mountain Coffee Roasters for trade practices with coffee bean farmers in Sumatra, Peru, and Mexico.

Other companies which made the list are Advanced Micro Devices, Inc. for its commitment to the community and employee well-being; and clothing retailer, Gap, Inc., for its honesty in reporting factory conditions. IBM has consistently made the list, as have Nike, Dell Corporation, and Motorola.

This notion of corporate social responsibility is a huge umbrella which covers many areas, including employee treatment, wages, and benefits, environmental awareness, diversity, investments, charitable contributions, community involvement, trading, endorsements, and in some cases political support.

What underlies these companies is a recognition and adherence to Socially Responsible Investing (SRI). SRI is not limited to a company-by-company investment strategy. In recent years, there has been an explosive growth in SRI Mutual Funds. These Funds have articulated their investment strategies which include specific social, economic, and in some cases, political objectives. They then do the work for the investor by selecting and monitoring a slate of companies whose own policies and goals resonate with the Fund. In 2006, many of these mutual funds far outpaced the overall market.

From www.financegoogle.com (January 12, 2007)

Symbol	Mutual Fund (Varied Size)	1 Year Annual Average 2006
CAAPX	Ariel Appreciation Fund	10.94%
DSEFX	Domini Social Equity Fund	12.58%
PRBLX	Parnassus Equity Income Fund	14.73%
MYPVX	Citizens Values Fund	15.95%
FLRUX	Flex-Funds Total Return Utilities	17.68%
BRSIX	Bridgeway Ultra Small Index	21.55%
PORTX	Portfolio 21: Progressive Invest Mngt.	24.38%
CWVGX	Calvert World Value Global Values FD	26.60%
NALFX	New Alternative Fund	33.82%

Compared to a successful S&P 500 Index D

Symbol	Mutual Fund (Varied Size)	1 Year Annual Average 2006
SBSDX	Legg Mason Partner S&P 500 Index D	15.66%

As a result, their decision reflects ethical consideration through a thoughtful deliberative process.

Employers aren't alone in their pursuit of an ethical workplace. In 2005, a survey jointly conducted by the public relations firm Fleishman-Hillard and the National Consumers League showed that 76 percent of American consumers stated that the way a company treats its employees is given a lot of weight in consumer purchasing decisions.

John D. Graham, CEO and Chairman of Fleishman-Hillard, points out that Americans have available more resources than ever to learn about companies and research their history of social responsibility. Graham gave the following summation of the survey results:

> *"What American consumers are telling us—perhaps influenced by ongoing coverage of corporate layoffs and employee benefit reductions—sheds new light on how we view corporate social responsibility. If companies want to maintain and strengthen their reputations, it will be essential for them to invest actively and visibly in their employees."*

Employees have also become very cognizant of the ethics of their potential employers. When ranking the most important factors when choosing an employer, the trend has reversed. In the past, finances and income were given the most weight when choosing an employer. Today, ethics and corporate responsibility are given more consideration than money by many. People want to be associated with companies that are fair and honest. They don't want to be associated with corruption and scandals. Employees who have worked at companies with questionable ethics have encountered difficulties finding other employment. Many Enron employees can vouch for the fact that their employment with Enron hurt their chances of obtaining work elsewhere, even if they were not involved or aware of any wrongdoings. Potential employees do their homework — they want to be proud of the company they work for.

Care2, a community network, recently conducted a survey of employees. Almost half (48%) of the respondents actually said they would take a job with a socially responsible company for less pay over an unethical company who would pay more. And, 40 percent said they would work longer and harder for a socially responsible organization.

Care2's survey also provided the following statistics:

- 73 percent of employees stated it is "very important" to work for a socially responsible company.
- 35 percent state they have terminated employment in the past because they felt the company they worked for was not ethical or socially responsible.

The ability to find and retain good employees is vital to any business. It's expensive to recruit, interview, and train new employees. Good employees who are obedient and loyal, and who care about their employer, produce quality work, which directly affects the quality of the goods and/or services they provide.

Also to be considered is cost savings. It is my experience that ethical companies reduce the risk of litigation, fines, and attorneys' fees for dishonesty, misrepresentation, unfair treatment of workers, unsafe environmental policies, and discriminatory practices. Countless companies have paid fines and attorney fees for their lack of responsibility and unethical behavior.

Let it suffice to say, billions of dollars in profits have been lost by corporations who have failed to assume and acknowledge the ethical responsibilities of obedience, loyalty, and care to their employees, shareholders, and communities. If companies were to instill the three principal duties of a fiduciary in every aspect of their businesses, ethical behavior and corporate responsibility would prevail over intentional or inadvertent wrongdoings.

Let us consider once again, Malden Mills. Clearly impressive is Aaron Feuerstein and his company in that they made an unprecedented move by paying thousands of employees a continual wage, even though they could not work after the factory was destroyed by fire. Of further significance is the fact that Feuerstein didn't even consider other, more lucrative, options for his company. Feuerstein was interviewed on CBS's 60 Minutes program in 2006. When asked why he just didn't keep the $300 million dollar insurance money, but chose to invest huge sums of it to keep his employees paid and insured, his response was "Well, it was the right thing to do."

And it was. In return, Feuerstein received a sincere amount of loyalty from his employees and the continuing gratitude of the community —a community which would have become a ghost town if his plant had moved overseas. He stayed in the community of Lawrence, and his employees stayed with him, working harder and longer hours to help him get the company back on its feet.

Feuerstein is now retired and the company has changed hands but his act while owner remains a source of inspiration to many. He has been the recipient of many awards for ethical leadership, including the 2005 Stanley C. Pace Leadership in Ethics Award by the Fellows of the Ethics Resource Center, a truly enviable legacy. Malden Mills' dedication and loyalty to its employees was not a matter of happenstance. Its mission statement has always said that Malden Mills will be a "caring and ethical corporation that benefits all of its stakeholders —its employees, its community, and its shareholders." Mr. Feuerstein recognized the duty of obedience and honored this agreement.

To Aaron Feuerstein, ethics were not just a policy on paper. They were practiced and stressed by both the company and its employees. Feuerstein didn't think what he did was such a big deal. His Mission Statement gave his community, shareholders, and employees his word. Then he kept it.

Chapter Fourteen

THE DECISION MAKING PROTOCOL
APPLIED

Earlier in the book, we were confronted with a challenging ethical dilemma involving a Juvenile Judge. Now let's apply our fiduciary protocols for successful ethical decision making. (You may wish to take a moment to glance back at the Judge's scenario in Chapter One).

To begin, we consider the duties of a fiduciary. As you recall, the obligations of a fiduciary are the duties of Obedience, Loyalty, and Care. With there being several potential starting points, I, as an attorney, feel compelled to address any potential legal implications first. Some jurisdictions have specifically addressed the act of suicide. In fact, some states consider the act a crime. Presumably, aiding and abetting a suicide might be considered a crime itself. Thus, if we're faced with this scenario, it would be wise to consider the potential criminal ramifications of our actions or inactions. Further, the rules of law are also keenly interested in the information related to a criminal act. The Judge's admission may require us to divulge this information to the appropriate authorities, particularly when disclosure could prevent a future crime. Specifically, there are several instances where the law could apply: the possible criminal act of suicide; the potential for future sexual abuse of children if the Judge does not commit suicide; perjury on the part of the Judge at his trial; or in general, the obstruction of justice.

Moving from the criminal implications, our analysis has likely prompted you to realize that there are several other legal implications as well. Namely, the written agreement or contract executed between the Judge and Reporter. As you recall, the Reporter agreed verbally, and in writing, not to publish the story before 5:00 p.m. the following day. This agreement may very well be in conflict with the laws of his jurisdiction or state. Also the question arises as to whether or not the Reporter had the authority to bind or obligate the newspaper, his employer, to any kind of agreement, especially one such as this.

The criminal and legal implications are not our only concerns. As the Reporter, we face professional implications as well. Here, we agreed in advance to certain limitations on publishing the story without knowing what the Judge might reveal. Generally, preliminary confidentiality arrangements or even payments for interviews are frowned upon by professional journalists. Moreover, our own agreement, in our role as the Reporter, creates the distinct possibility of making the story inconsequential by waiting until the next day to print it. Many if not most professions have a Code of Conduct or Code of Ethics which serves as a standard for professional conduct and which are designed to assist members of that profession with difficult professional and ethical challenges like this one. The Society of Professional Journalists has a Code of Ethics for its members which provides guidance as to the degree of care that would be used by a Journalist of ordinary prudence under the same or similar circumstances.

The Society of Professional Journalists Code of Ethics states that a reporter must, "**Seek the truth and report it**." (see complete code of ethics at www.spj.org/ethicscode.asp). It further advises:

> *Journalists should be honest, fair and courageous in gathering, reporting and interpreting information.* www.spj.org/ethicscode.asp

This same Code of Ethics admonishes reporters to, "**minimize harm**." to those who are involved or are the subject of reporting. This is especially true when reporting about victims of sex crimes.

> *Ethical journalists treat sources, subjects and colleagues as human beings deserving of respect.* www.spj.org/ethicscode.asp

Obviously, a reporter's deviation from this Code could invite serious professional consequences.

In the following section, I have put myself in the Reporter's shoes, to demonstrate how I would answer the questions and apply the successful ethical decision making protocol.

Consideration of the criminal, legal and professional implications of this dilemma naturally lead us to the first prong of successful ethical decision making, or the Duty of Obedience.

Obedience: The duty requires a fiduciary to act in accordance with agreed to contracts, governing documents as well as all applicable laws and regulations.

In order to determine the Duty of Obedience we ask ourselves the following questions. The answers to these four questions may not immediately give us a solution, but we will have some initial clarity about our commitments.

1.   ***What did I agree to do?***
     I agreed not to publish the story or discuss the interview with anyone until after 5:00 p.m. the following day.

2.   ***What did I say I would do?***
     I said I would not publish the story or discuss the interview with anyone until 5:00 p.m. the following day.

3.   ***What are the understood expectations of this agreement for me?***
     The understood expectations of this agreement are that I will neither discuss nor publish the story until 5:00 p.m. the following day. It was clear from the Judge's statement that he understood that I would not interfere with his threatened suicide or report any information to law enforcement before 5:00 p.m. the following day. In exchange I was given the exclusive on his story.

4.   ***Is the agreement legal?***
     Right now, I don't know. I did not really think about the legality of the agreement at the time I made it!

This fourth question makes the Duty of Obedience a lot more complex. What we said we would do and what we agreed to do as it relates to the Judge seems pretty clear, but whether or not it is proper under the law in not so clear.

As the reporter, we agreed to the Judge's terms before we knew he was intending to commit suicide and admitted he was a child molester. Considering these two very salient issues, it should prompt us to think about what our obligations are under the law. Does the law require us to report the Judge's threat of suicide or prevent it ourselves? Does the law require us to report the Judge's admission of sexual misconduct immediately upon learning such information? Do we believe the Judge will follow through on his threat of suicide? And if not, does the Judge pose some potential risk in the future? Right now, these are all questions for which we do not have answers. What we do know is that the Duty of Obedience requires us to follow all applicable laws, regulations and governing documents. We also know obedience mandates that our decisions and actions must be lawful; otherwise they cannot be ethical as a fiduciary.

Frankly, our agreement with the Judge may be in conflict with the law and may serve to undermine the very purpose of the interview. This uncertainty naturally leads us to the second prong of the successful ethical decision making protocol, or the Duty of Loyalty.

Loyalty: Being steadfast in allegiance to a person, ideal or custom.

Loyalty changes our priorities, steering them away from ourselves to other people or causes. It means that we consider how our actions or decisions affect someone else's best interest rather than our own. I think for any person who is in the role of a fiduciary, whether that role is a mother or a veteran reporter, as in this dilemma, it is only natural that we think about the people who are involved and what obligation we owe to these people. As the Reporter, who is acting as a fiduciary, I must place the interests of others first, so obviously I will appear last on my list of people to consider.

1. ***Who is involved?***
    - *The Judge*
    - *The victims and potential victims of the Judge's actions*
    - *The Public*
    - *The Newspaper who employs the Reporter*
    - *Law enforcement*
    - *Myself (The Reporter)*

2. ***Of those involved, what is my obligation to each?***
    - *The Judge: I owe an obligation to the Judge because of the agreement. I may owe an obligation to the Judge to prevent his suicide. Likely, the Judge feels my obligation is to "let him be" as per our agreement.*
    - *Victims and potential victims of the Judge's actions: The Code of Ethics requires me to **"minimize harm"** to those who are involved or the subject of my reports. This is especially true when*

*reporting on victims of sex crimes and minors. In this situation,
I have minors who have also been victims of sex crimes. Clearly,
I owe an obligation to these victims, their families and any
potential victims of the Judge.*

- *The Public: The Society of Professional Journalists Code of
Ethics states with great clarity that a reporter must, "**Seek the
truth and report it.**" I owe an obligation to the Public. In fact,
the Code of Ethics suggests it is to the Public that I may owe
the highest obligation. The very essence of my profession as a
journalist is to "**seek the truth and report it.**"*

- *The Newspaper (my employer): What obligation, if any, is
owed to the paper? As the Reporter, I owe the same obligation
to the newspaper as I would to any employer. I must conduct
my work within the guidelines I have agreed to as a condition
of my employment. Likely, the newspaper's goal is the same as
mine, which is to seek the truth and report it and to get that
truth out as soon as possible with minimum harm. As a result,
there is some obligation to the paper.*

- *Law enforcement: As a reporter, I am also a citizen who now
has some very sensitive information which the law may require
me to divulge, sooner rather than later. This is a duty I have as a
citizen <u>and</u> a reporter. A duty that may very well require me to
have some obligation to the law and law enforcement to report
what I learned from the Judge <u>before</u> publication.*

- *Myself (the Reporter): As the Reporter, what obligation do I
owe to myself? If I am intent upon acting as a true fiduciary,
my sole concern is with others. But, I too am human. I want to
publish an exclusive and high profile story.*

The process of identifying all the people involved and all the
potentially conflicting obligations doesn't resolve our dilemma. But at
a minimum, it does establish the people who we may affect with our
decision and what our obligations are to each. This is an important
accomplishment. Without asking the questions, we may overlook
someone.

While we have examined our obligations to the people involved
the same unanswered questions that could have criminal, legal and
professional ramifications remain.

*Does the law require us to report the Judge's threat of suicide or even prevent
it ourselves?*

Does the law require us to report the Judge's admission of sexual misconduct immediately upon learning such information?

Do we believe that the Judge will follow through on his threat, and if not, does the Judge pose some potential risk in the future?

Is it proper to breach our contract and break our word to the Judge if the agreement conflicts with the law or other obligations?

These are all questions for which we do not have answers. We need these answers to make a successful ethical decision. If we don't know the answers to these critical questions, then it is incumbent upon us to determine if we are in a position to move forward with this decision on our own or seek the counsel or advice of a third party. When we make agreements which possibly conflict with governing documents and applicable laws and this conflict affects others, we must conclude that we are not in a position to resolve the dilemma on our own.

Upon reaching this point, we engage the third prong of successful ethical decision making, which is the fiduciary Duty of Care. If you recall, Duty of Care means that a person must use the care "an ordinarily prudent person would use in the same or similar circumstance" otherwise known as "The prudent person rule." Fortunately, the Duty of Care is flexible and allows us not only to seek assistance and knowledge from others, but also expects us to use our knowledge, experience, instinct and insights. It is also this flexibility that allows us to shift the order we ask the questions to fit the unique dilemma in which we are involved. The Duty of Care prompts us to ask four questions which are as follows:

1. ***Am I in a position to decide this on my own?***
   No. I don't know the law as it pertains to the Judge's admission or his threatened suicide. Further, I do not know the paper's position on honoring or dishonoring my agreement with the Judge.

If we are not in a position to decide this problem on our own, then we must ask ourselves the following:

2. ***Where do I find the answer?***
   - *Senior Editor/Supervisor: I think any reasonable and prudent reporter who is attempting to use good judgment and common sense would recognize that talking to the Senior Editor of his newspaper would be a likely place to start. Typically, any Senior Editor of an established newspaper is a professional who has considerable experience and who has likely faced many similar dilemmas in the*

past. The Editor can also advise as to the position of the newspaper regarding this dilemma. No matter what my ultimate decision, the Editor will let me know whether or not the paper will stand behind me and my agreement with the Judge, whether I choose to honor the agreement or break it. The Editor will also certainly recommend a conversation with the newspaper's General Counsel or Attorney.

- *Attorney: A consultation with an attorney is wise on several fronts. The attorney can advise as to whether or not the law requires an intervention in the Judge's threatened suicide. The Attorney can further advise as to whether or not the admission of the Judge's sexual misconduct requires me to contact law enforcement immediately with the knowledge I now possess. An attorney will also be able to advise me as to whether or not the admission by the Judge and his threatened suicide would somehow invalidate the terms of the contract that I signed with the Judge.*

- *Spiritual advisor: As a person of faith, this dilemma may possess an even greater challenge. It may be necessary to consult with a spiritual or religious advisor as to what moral obligation rests with the victims, the Judge and the public's right to know. Ultimately, the question remains to whom do I owe the obligation? Prioritizing the obligations based upon faith is essentially a decision one must make premised upon one's own faith or creed.*

- *Myself: There is one other intangible not to be overlooked in my decision making, and that is my own instinct. Do I believe the judge will commit suicide? Or was it a tactic for other ends? Further, do I believe the Judge will have access to other potential victims either prior to his suicide or during the continuation of his trial? Do I believe the Judge would harm others after his seemingly sincere regret of prior misconduct? In other words what does my instinct tell me? My instinct will likely quicken the pace of my actions.*

The next question I ask myself is:

3. **Do I have the authority to make this decision?**
    I return again to the Facts. The Judge called me for an interview. No one else heard the Judge's confession to my knowledge. No one else signed the agreement. No one else is aware of the pending suicide. The newspaper may argue that I cannot contractually bind them, but I am the paper's representative and they are now in this situation, like it or not. Clearly, the decision as to whether or not to divulge the story before or after 5:00 p.m., calling the authorities, preventing

the suicide or honoring the agreement is now mine to make and mine alone.

We may not have asked for this dilemma but we are in it. Even if the paper pulled away from us because of the agreement or circumstances, we can still divulge the information to others. The facts and circumstances of this dilemma give us the authority to make this decision, if nothing else.

The final question I must ask myself is as follows:

4.   ***What is in the best interests of those for whom I am making the decision?***

There remains one critical but unanswered question from the duty of obedience. Am I mandated by law to report the Judge's admission of sexual misconduct or planned suicide? In my particular case, I apply Texas law. Texas law is not too clear on the suicide issue, but Texas law is quite clear that I must report both past sexual misconduct by the Judge as well as any knowledge of future misconduct by the Judge to law enforcement. This law strongly suggests that my agreement with the Judge is illegal.[4]

The Duty of Obedience mandates I follow the law. A decision cannot be ethical if it is illegal. Therefore, under the law of my jurisdiction, I am obligated to report the Judge's admission of sexual misconduct to law enforcement before publication.

I believe this decision of honoring the law is in the best interest of those for whom I am making the decision, despite any legal and professional consequences to me. In this instance, for me, the law determined the priority of my obligations. This mandatory prioritization under the law is not uncommon. Here, the best interest of the victims, potential victims and law enforcement come first. The Judge, newspaper and I come last.

However, I broke my word. I dishonored myself by entering an illegal agreement which I made in haste so that I could obtain an exclusive and high profile story — a selfish decision.

It is important to note here that different people, even you, may have different responses to each question. There is no absolute "correct" answer but if you use the protocol there is a "right" answer for each of us. Your answer is your own.

In summary, I believe there are three results which are more probable than others as to how this dilemma will end. These results primarily evolve from our duties under the principle of obedience. The first result derives from a legal duty to report the Judge's misconduct or pending suicide. Earlier, the protocol advised we consult an attorney for advice on the laws of this jurisdiction. If the laws of this jurisdiction require that we report or intervene in the Judge's threat of suicide then we must do so despite what we understood from the agreement with the Judge. If you recall from Chapter 9, the Duty of Obedience requires that any agreement be legal under all applicable laws, regulations and governing documents. Here, in his zeal to get to an exclusive story, the Reporter rushed his decision making. He did so to get something he wanted. Quite easily, a prudent, thoughtful reporter could have simply stated, "I will agree to your terms if they do not require me to break the law or my profession's Code of Ethics." As noted earlier, a fiduciary's actions and decisions must be lawful, otherwise they cannot be ethical as a fiduciary. It was the Reporter's rushed decision making that put him and his newspaper in this position.

The same conclusion is true for the Judge's admission of misconduct. If the law requires us to report this information to law enforcement then we should do so. An act cannot be ethical if illegal. The Reporter did make a rushed, ill advised and illegal agreement, but we are legally obligated to report the Judge's admission and should do so immediately. The Reporter gave his word to the Judge and maintains some obligation to the Judge. An ethical reporter, in my view, should contact the Judge and inform him that the law requires his admission of misconduct to be reported to the Police. It is ethical and honorable to admit our mistake to the Judge and be truthful about what has to be done now that we know what the law requires in this situation. We made a deal so if we break it, at minimum, we should tell the Judge of our intent. The Judge or his family may sue under the agreement, but there are consequences when we make rushed decisions like this one and lawsuits are frequently such a consequence. However, being truthful, direct and accountable are attributes of any fiduciary. The Reporter has a duty "to seek the truth and report it." This will happen regardless of the Judge's action. Preventing the suicide and reporting the admission to the authorities does NOT prevent the story from being published. The Reporter can still turn the story over to the paper. If the newspaper does not allow the publication due to this unfortunate mess, then that is their decision not ours. We made the effort.

Earlier in this book, we talked about the importance of honoring our word and keeping it. This principle is no less important now. Here, our word was premised on an illegal agreement which the law did not allow us to honor. This demonstrates that our future agreements must be premised upon a full understanding of what we are agreeing to do and thoughtful, deliberate diligence must be used before making such agreements. The Duty of Care mandates such an approach if we are to avoid problems such as this one.

In my view, there is a second probable outcome which also depends greatly on the Duty of Obedience. If the laws of our jurisdiction or state do not mandate or require us to report or prevent the Judge's pending suicide nor divulge his admission of sexual misconduct, our circumstances change significantly. Here, we are under no legal or criminal obligation to report either. The duty to "seek the truth and report it" is not conflicting with any law. If this is the case, our agreement with the Judge can be honored, hence we keep our word. We are able to report the story within the terms of the contract and conform to a reporter's duty to inform the public. These two obligations are met without potential legal reprisals from the Judge or his estate. As noted earlier, a fiduciary should honor agreements unless they are illegal.

The third probable outcome has bearing on the prior two scenarios because it involves the spiritual and moral beliefs of the Reporter. Simply applying the laws of the local jurisdiction may not suffice for some people. The compelling facts of the Judge's pending suicide or his potential threat to others may in the opinion of some be governed by Divine Law. Again, we are afflicted by the rushed decision making of the Reporter. If our religion, faith or spiritual creed cannot allow us to stand by while another commits suicide, then we should inform the Judge of our position. Whether it is at the time of his revelation of his intent to commit suicide or later, the Judge should know of our intent to intervene. A fiduciary should be direct and accountable at all times and letting the Judge know our intent is consistent with our role.

The same is true as to the Judge's admission of sexual misconduct. If our religion, faith or spiritual creed demands reporting the Judge to authorities then we should do so. Again, our governing document may be divine and not legislative, but we still have some obligation to the Judge. As such, we should inform the Judge of our position and be prepared to deal with any potential legal consequences of breaching the agreement. It should be noted that in the case where the agreement is not illegal and the law requires no duty to report, any legal reprisals made by the Judge or his estate could have more force. It is also important to note that we will be in violation of what is likely a legal agreement with the Judge, therefore we are likely not entitled to print the story. Since we are breaching the agreement, we cannot ethically print the story. Here, we should instruct the Judge that we are not honoring the agreement and give him the opportunity to tell his story to another reporter. By conducting ourselves in this fashion, we can honor our faith or spiritual creed, allow the Judge to tell the story to another reporter hence allowing the other reporter to "seek the truth and report it." Indirectly, but significantly, we honor our obligation to the Public.

In any event, any of the scenarios or decisions that are made above can be the best solution depending upon the circumstances. There is much we don't know from this situation, but it is intrinsically the responsibility of fiduciaries to make sure that they learn the facts as best they are able as they exercise their duties. Or from the perspective of this book, we prudently and thoughtfully deliberate on each prong of the fiduciary protocol.

The scenario is purposely fraught with legal, moral, professional, and financial consequences. Further, it is a situation with rapidly approaching deadlines. For many, including myself, these exigent variables can create stress. The mind begins to move rapidly and the pace of our actions picks up. Despite the time constraints and conflicts, we do ourselves no favor by deciding too quickly. In fact, a decision too quickly made runs counter to the fiduciary's duties. Though decisions may vary, the proper ones are arrived at through employing the protocols here described. At minimum, we availed ourselves and those involved to as much time for thoughtful and considered deliberation as we can muster considering all our obligations.

As is evident, there are innumerable variables, circumstances, and consequences included with any ethical dilemma. Our decision does not have to be correct one hundred percent of the time. But, we must be diligent in the process. As I tell my clients and students, after the decision is made, we need to be able to demonstrate a thoughtful, sensible reason as to why we made the decision. This protocol provides just such a method.

CONCLUSION

We are all creatures of habit. This morning, I got up and started the coffee pot and walked to the front door to pick up the <u>Houston Chronicle</u>, just like I did yesterday, and just like I'll do tomorrow. Then, I sat down, drank my coffee, and caught up on the news.

Just like yesterday, I read about corporate and political corruption and fraud. I read about criminal activity here in Houston and across the country. Corporate bankruptcies and layoffs get their usual space. I read a story about a large U.S. corporation announcing a layoff to 300 of its workers via e-mail.

Yes, even though I am inundated with media and news coverage, there is still an occasional piece of news that can illicit some shock value from me. I now realize that I am not totally numb to the wrongdoings and injustices which have become more commonplace. I thought about how those 300 workers must have felt when they received news of this magnitude in such a cold and impersonal manner. Can we learn from this? Is there a better way? Obviously, I believe, no, I know there is a better way. And, I trust you do too.

We, like my students, are creatures of habit, products of our environment, and the sum of our experiences. Part of their experience is my class and now having read this book, some of my class has become part of your experience, too.

I started this endeavor to help articulate a guide for the not always easy process of ethical decision making. As a result, I arrived upon the three principles of Obedience, Loyalty, and Care. Obedience, Loyalty, and Care are theoretical concepts, but they bring real and tangible results. What started as a guide for students grew into a protocol based upon concepts that can be applied almost universally. We live in a time of constant change and fast-paced living. The economy, technology, and laws change almost daily. It is almost impossible to keep up with all the changes. Given this fact, we all need a reliable method for making ethical decisions even if there are uncertainties and conflict.

As I teach these three principles to my students and others, it is my hope that they can use them to determine the next right thing to do. I firmly believe that you will find them helpful as well.

Endnotes

[1] This is a fictional story not based upon any specific incident. The events described are, however, plausible and constructed to provide a challenging ethical circumstance.

[2] Ex Parte Crow Dog, 109 U.S. 556, 3 S. Ct. 396, 27 L. Ed. 1030 (1883)

[3] See **www.corpedia.com** for more information

[4] Texas Family Code, Chapter 261; Texas Penal Code §7.02(3)

APPENDIX I

Key Terms

Fiduciary:
Derived from the Latin term meaning "holding in trust". As a noun, it refers to a person to whom property or power is entrusted for the benefit of another. The primary duties of a fiduciary are "Obedience", "Loyalty", and "Care".

Obedience:
To act in accordance with agreed to contracts, governing documents as well as all applicable laws and regulations.

Loyalty:
To remain steadfast in allegiance to a person, ideal or custom.

Care:
To use the concern an ordinarily prudent person would use under the same or similar circumstances.

Deliberate:
To think about or discuss issues and decisions carefully; to think about deliberately and often with formal discussion before reaching a decision.

Prudent:
Latin term marked by wisdom or judiciousness; shrewd in the management of practical affairs and marked by circumspection.

Integrity:
Doing the right thing, even when you are afraid.

APPENDIX II

Working Through the Questions

I. Obedience

1. What did I agree to do?
2. What did I say I would do?
3. What are the understood expectations of this agreement for me?
4. Is this agreement legal?

II. Loyalty

1. Who is involved?
2. Of those involved, what is my obligation to each?

III. Care

1. What is in the best interest of the persons for whom I am making the decision?
2. Am I in a position to decide this on my own?
3. Where do I find the answer?
4. Do I have the authority to make this decision?

About Critical Communications, LLC

Critical Communications, LLC is a corporate training, speaking and seminar resource company, led by Michael Tate Barkley and Steve Bain, that is dedicated to helping organizations of all sizes foster ethical and socially responsible corporate cultures. Their programs provide participants with the tools needed to move beyond simply meeting the requirements stated in the Sarbanes-Oxley Act and other statutes. They teach proven protocols that help participants adopt an attitude of ethics which in turn becomes an integral part of the organization's culture.

An accomplished expert in the development of ethical corporate cultures and effective communications, Michael Tate Barkley is both a dynamic and engaging speaker and a highly sought after trainer with a wonderful ability to inform and inspire audiences to develop and apply a personal code of ethics in order to achieve their goals. Tate has been a practicing attorney for more than 16 years. He is also an Assistant Instructional Professor for the University of Houston School of Communications. Tate has been trained by the American Society of Training and Development (ASTD) and is a Certified Prejudice

Reduction Trainer with the National Coalition Building Institute (NCBI). Tate's seminars are filled with the humor and lighthearted teaching style that has become his trademark.

Steve Bain is a leading expert in the fields of fraud investigation and prevention and ethical behavior. He is an energetic and compelling speaker and trainer in high demand for his ability to inform and motivate audiences to develop corporate cultures that prevent corrupt behavior. Steve is a Certified Forensic Interviewer and an Associate Member of the National Association of Certified Fraud Examiners. A seasoned trial lawyer with 18 years experience, Steve knows how to use humor and pop culture references to connect with audiences and involve them in the learning process.

For more information or to contact us please visit our website at
www.criticalcommunications.org

Endnotes

[1] This is a fictional story not based upon any specific incident. The events described are, however, plausible and constructed to provide a challenging ethical circumstance.

[2] Ex Parte Crow Dog, 109 U.S. 556, 3 S. Ct. 396, 27 L. Ed. 1030 (1883)

[3] See **www.corpedia.com** for more information

[4] Texas Family Code, Chapter 261; Texas Penal Code §7.02(3)